MERLE HODGE was born in 1944 in Trinidad and Tobago. She read French at University College, London, where she did postgraduate work on francophone Caribbean and African writers. She has taught at secondary and tertiary institutions across the Caribbean. At present, she teaches English and Creative Writing at the Trinidad campus of the University of the West Indies.

Crick Crack, Monkey was first published in 1970. Merle Hodge is also the author of *For the Life of Laetitia* (Farrar, Straus and Giroux, 1993, and Orion Children's Books, 1995). She has published short stories and numerous articles in Caribbean and international journals.

MERLE HODGE

CRICK CRACK, MONKEY

Introduction by Roy Narinesingh
University of West Indies

Heinemann

Heinemann Educational Publishers
Halley Court, Jordan Hill, Oxford OX2 8EJ
A part of Harcourt Education Limited

Heinemann: A Division of Reed Publishing (USA) Inc.
361 Hanover Street, Portsmouth, NH 03801–3912, USA

OXFORD   MELBOURNE   AUCKLAND
JOHANNESBURG   KUALA LUMPUR   GABORONE
PORTSMOUTH (NH) USA   CHICAGO

First published by André Deutsch Ltd 1970
First published in Caribbean Writers Series 1981
This edition first published 2000

British Library Cataloguing in Publication Data
A catalogue record for this book is available from the British Library.

Library of Congress Cataloging-in-Publication Data
Hodge, Merle.
    Crick crack, monkey / Merle Hodge.
        p.   cm. — (African writers series)
    ISBN 0-435-98951-0
    I. Title. II. Series.
  PR9320.9.K56K53   0000
  823 — dc21   98-9591
                          CIP

Cover design by Touchpaper
Cover illustration by Steve Rawlings

Phototypeset by SetSystems Ltd, Saffron Walden, Essex
Printed and bound in Great Britain by Cox and Wyman Ltd,
Reading, Berkshire

ISBN 0 435 98951 0

03 04 05 6 5 4

for Marmee

and to my God-Children
Luzia, of Africa, and Mark, of the West Indies
and to the Children's Home Egelundshuset,
Denmak

Introduction

Crick Crack, Monkey, which was first published in 1970, belongs to a group of West Indian novels, such as *The Year in San Fernando* and *Christopher* which deal with the theme of childhood. The central character, Tee, moves in two worlds – the world of Tantie and the world of Aunt Beatrice – and those two worlds are bound together in a coherent and unified way by the response of the central character, who is also narrator, to the experiences of both worlds. The child, Tee, moves in a context in which there is strong opposition between certain social and cultural values and, as narrator, she recounts the intensely personal dilemmas of her life in that context. This she does with a remarkable depth of insight and with a vivid evocation of childhood memories. The reader is made to share in the diversity and richness of Tee's experiences without being able to discern at times where the child's voice with a child's perception of things slides into the adult voice and vision of the omniscient author. Child vision and adult vision are made to coalesce at several points in the novel.

The two worlds of childhood which Tee inhabits result from the nature of her domestic circumstances. Her father, who has emigrated to England, is the brother of Tantie, and her deceased mother is sister to Aunt Beatrice. Tee oscillates between these two spheres of existence and emerges as a deeply disturbed being – a plight derived from the essential conflict of life styles between creole middle-class and Tantie's world. The conflict externalized in these two classes of society generates acute feelings of ambivalence within Tee. Both in form and content the novel is indeed a response to the inner pressures of a profoundly felt and complex experience. The vivid exploration of the child's inner world confers on the novel its essential strength. The child's feelings, thoughts and actions, as she responds to the social and cultural environment in which the novel is set, reflect the authenticity of remembered experience. It is pertinent to examine at this point how the movement of the novel both in time and place is integral to Tee's growth.

Tee's early years are passed amidst scenes of hilarity, aggression, warmth and childish rapture. This period of growing up in Tantie's world is presented with freshness, vivacity and charm:

> Tantie's company was loud and hilarious and the intermittent squawk and flurry of mirth made me think of the fowl-run when something fell into the midst of the fat hens. (p. 4)

Tantie (jealously) aggressively asserts her right of guardianship of both Tee and her little brother, Toddan. When she wins out on the issue she recalls in colloquially vigorous language:

> 'Well she know big-shot, yu know, big-shot in all kinda Government office, Father-priest and thing – so she get this paper. But we wipe we backside with she paper – we send the chirren to get some town-breeze, an' in that time I get a statement from Selwyn – yu shoulda see the bitch face in the Courthouse! Eh! she face look like if she panty fall-down!' There was an attack of hilarity. 'Eh! but that is the end of that bitch, matter fix, yu livin' by yu Tantie, yu father self could go to Hell – wha yu say, allyu ain't even have no use for he!' and we clambered closer about her, all but strangling her, so that she squawked again. (p. 43)

The fight for guardianship of these two children is consistently a point of reference in the novel. In fact it generates the oppositions between the world of Tantie and Aunt Beatrice, revealing the quality of life in those two cultural and social classes.

The boisterousness, elemental toughness and rebellion – characteristic of this first phase of Tee's upbringing – grow spontaneously out of the quality of life within Tantie's environment. The rich, solid texture of life is intimately apprehended through scenes shot through with realistic details. Tee's memories of these earlier days are recorded with remarkable fidelity. One feels that Tee really belongs to that world. The vigorous style with which experiences are presented reveals a sureness of grasp and an extraordinary delicacy of insight. At times the prose achieves a fluidity and flexibility of rhythm enacting an energy of life and a closeness to the rhythms of speech:

> Tantie raged all evening. An' she had a mind not to give us anything to eat because allyu belly must be done full wid that bitch ice-cream and sweetie. She raged and rampaged with no indication of subsiding, so that Mikey finally got up and left the house with a loud cheups; she called down curses on his departing figure and then returned to Auntie Beatrice and our escapade. She reiterated for the hundredth time what could have happened to us: 'we had jus' nearly get we arse kidnap'! And then the thought of it became uncontainable; she flew at me and battered me with the dishcloth she had in her hand, hitting out in furious relief. (p. 14)

During the August vacation at her grandmother's, Ma, Tee moves through an 'enchanted country'. The joys of early childhood – children's games, fruit picking, walks – are presented effectively through images of sound, sight, scent and movement. The child's sensibility is fully alert to the natural world:

> And there were the days of real rain. We could see it coming, down across the water, a dark ceiling letting down slow grey streamers into the horizon (that was God pee-peeing into his posie) and then it would be pounding the earth like a thousand horses coming at us through the trees. It was frightening and exciting. (p. 18)

> We walked behind her squelching joyously in the new puddles and mud. The air smelt brown and green, like when the earth was being made. From a long way off the river was calling to us through the trees, in one continuous groan, so that when we finally came to it, wet and splashed from the puddles and from the bushes we had brushed against, it was as though we had been straining along in it the whole time. (p. 20)

It is in contrast to the world of Tantie's household. We do not hear Tantie's exclamations, expletives, or the raucousness and hilarity of her company. It is significant to note that this period of Tee's life is filled with feelings and thoughts of pure delight and sustenance.

Another phase of Tee's life, which takes up a significant part of the novel, but integral to the central theme, is the experience of schooling. Her initial response to the world of school is one of animated expectancy:

> I looked forward to school. I looked forward to the day when I could pass my hand swiftly from side to side on a blank piece of paper leaving meaningful marks in its wake; to staring nonchalantly into a book until I turned over the

page, a gesture pregnant with importance for it indicated that one had not merely been staring, but that that most esoteric of processes had been taking place whereby the paper had yielded up something or other as a result of having been stared at. (p. 22)

But this expectation is soon dashed, when on her first encounter with school, recess is announced by Mrs Hinds. Through Tee's eyes, we get satiric glimpses on the practice of schooling. Rigid conformity, emphasis on external order, unquestioning obedience, submissiveness and passivity, the irrelevance of the curriculum (both cultural and linguistic), the absence of stimulation to learn, and lack of warmth all reflect the evils of schooling derived from imported metropolitan conceptions of education. School, in fact, is no more than 'a grim, joyless place', with a 'pervading atmosphere of unreality and disorientation'. The authorial voice lies behind the presentation of these facets of school life; but the tone is not of harsh comment but subtle and civilized disapproval. There is levity but with an underlying seriousness. There is mild ridicule but not without an awareness of what ought to be. The values and attitudes transmitted through schooling run counter to growth, mutilate sensibilities – are destructive of a sense of self and opposed to creativity. In fact, Tee's assumed double, Helen, synthesizes the nature of the psychological damage done by the nature of school experience within the novel.

Tee's winning of the scholarship at The Exhibition Examination becomes the occasion for her full entry into the world of Aunt Beatrice. Tantie, however, does not give up the battle. She firmly refuses Aunt Beatrice's offer of uniform for Tee:

'Well thank you Madam, but we will see about that,' replied Tantie sharply, 'we are not paupers.' (p. 76)

Tee leaves (for the world of Aunt Beatrice) Tantie's world with its solid intimacies – 'Tee Darling, Tee dou-dou', its rich and varied texture of life, a life sustaining and delightful, resonant with the exuberance of childhood energy, unvarnished but accommodating. Her initiation into the negro middle-class is a very uneasy one. The artificiality of Aunt Beatrice's home with its formalities, conventions, false pretensions, is exposed by an incisive consciousness. At once we begin to experience, through Tee's eyes, the attitudes and values which divide the worlds of Tantie and Aunt Beatrice. Tee feels alienated by discriminations of colour and class. Her consciousness constantly shifts and assumes a complexity borne out of her exposure to two differing life styles. Through vivid characterization of Aunt Beatrice and Tantie the contrast of both social and cultural systems is carefully delineated. This period of Tee's life can be described as intensely painful. It is well to note that the nature of her experience is now more complex and certainly fraught with uncertainties, doubts and self-questioning. The pattern of to and fro movement on the physical plane finds correspondence in the shifting consciousness of Tee – as she experiences ambivalent feelings towards both worlds. Her discord of mind and of heart is intensified by her remembrance of days gone by, and her present wish for acceptability in an alien world:

> I wanted to shrink, to disappear. Sometimes I thought I
> would gladly live under the back steps with Dash, rather
> than cross their paths all day long. I felt that the very sight
> of me was an affront to common decency. I wished that
> my body could shrivel up and fall away, that I could step
> out new and acceptable. (p. 107)

The verbs 'shrivel', 'shrink', 'disappear' express the intensity of Tee's death wish – for complete rebirth, self-annihilation, for transformation of self. She resented Tantie bitterly but at the same time she expressed shame and distress to find herself thinking in this way:

> At times I resented Tantie bitterly for not having let Auntie Beatrice get us in the first place and bring us up properly. What Auntie Beatrice said so often was quite true: how could a woman with no sense of right and wrong take it upon herself to bring up children, God knew the reason why He hadn't given her any of her own. And I was ashamed and distressed to find myself thinking of Tantie in this way. (p. 107)

Tee's consciousness now receives a much fuller exploration. Essentially we are invited to share in the exploration of the mind of Tee – a consciousness bewildered by her removal from a society suffused with warmth, affection, naturalness, neighbourliness and fellow-feeling to one marked by its false notions of gentility, affectation, and a denial of humane feeling. The terrible dislocation which she feels is psychological. The feelings of rejection, scorn, alienation which assail her in her new society, both at Aunt Beatrice's home and at school, make her examine herself in a new light, through values and attitudes imposed by this new world:

> Auntie Beatrice announced her firm intention to haul me out of what she termed alternately my ordinaryness and my niggeryness. (p. 105)

The word 'haul' powerfully suggests the violent and unnatural means of Aunt Beatrice's intentions. At church, Tee describes the nature of her discomfort:

. . . the whole atmosphere seemed to be one of reproof, of trial; it was if the whole church, people and building, were coldly regarding me, waiting to pull me up when I fell out of line. (p. 86)

She is repelled by her Aunt's perpetual smile, the exaggerated importance she gives to knife and fork in eating, her discriminatory attitude to 'coolies and niggers', her emphasis on form and status. However, Tee eventually begins to adopt this style of life – not without intense feelings of shame, guilt and remorse. The denial of her past and her assimilation into the middle-class are reflected in her shifting moods. As she becomes fully integrated into the world of Aunt Beatrice her words and actions reflect the very values and attitudes which at first horrified her. The prospect of a visit from Tantie distresses her. Memories of home bring shame and embarrassment. The acquaintances of her early childhood are now 'raucous niggery people', 'coolies'. Tantie's visit produces in her feelings of shame and distress. She resents Tantie bitterly 'for not having Auntie Beatrice get us in the first place and bring us up properly':

If I had never lived there, if Auntie Beatrice had whisked us away from the very beginning and brought us here, then I would have been nice. (p. 110)

On her return to bid farewell to Tantie before her departure abroad, she is openly repelled by Tantie's naturalness, and hates to be associated with it:

The night before we left the macommès and compès filled the house, come to drink a little one on us. But macommès and compès are never known to stop at a little one, and the usual gaiety ensued, in which we the pretext were quite

forgotten. Which was just as well, for I sat in a corner
shrinking from the ordinaryness of it all, until Mr Joseph
pounced on me. (p. 123)

Tee becomes a victim of Aunt Beatrice's frustrated hopes in her
children. It is ironical that Aunt Beatrice should be critical of
Tantie's method of bringing up children and yet cling so tena-
ciously to one who has been partly brought up by her. After Tee
enters the world of the middle-class she never knows the kind of
happiness she experienced in her earlier days. In fact, personal
dilemmas become intense:

Everything was changing, unrecognizable, pushing me out.
This was as it should be, since I had *moved up* and no
longer had any place here. But it was *painful* and I longed
all the more to be on my way.(p. 122)

She underlines the inevitability of her position; but the choice
which Tee makes, her commitment to middle-class respectability
can only lead to the erosion of her self-worth and personal
dignity. She will continue to experience inner dissonance because
the happy past which she has known intimately will continue to
intrude. The novel does not suggest a resolution of her dilemma.
Since Tee coalesces two worlds – those of Tantie and Auntie
Beatrice, her conflicts will be indefinite. Withdrawal from the
situation by her emigration to England is not a morally affirma-
tive position, for reconciliation can only be achieved by a mature
revaluation of her condition. For Tee, personal synthesis and
coherence are still to be achieved.

Inherent in the moral structure of the novel is the falsity of
her position. Auntie Beatrice and Tee, in varying degrees, are
victims of self-deception. Auntie Beatrice has reaped the ills that
derive from her false pretensions – a disintegrated family life –

hollow and meaningless. Her disappointment grew out of the very values she cultivated in her children:

> 'You see the family I got! Spend my life teaching my children to be decent, teaching them what is important, and then they forget who it was that got them where they are.'(p. 102)

Beneath the veneer of gentility and respectability lie the corrupting forces undermining family life and relationships – the denial of that liberal mind and generosity of heart which transcend race and class – a liberality so abundantly evident in Tantie and her associates.

ROY NARINESINGH
School of Education
University of the West Indies
St Augustine

NOTE Study questions are provided on page 124.

1

We had posted ourselves at the front window, standing on a chair. Tantie said we were stupid, for they might not come back till next morning or maybe even for days but if we wanted to stand on tiptoe at the window for a week that was all right by her as long as we got down once in a while to bathe.

At every movement in the street we craned our necks – no, it was only Mr Henry.

'Mr Henry!' we shrieked, 'we gettin a baby!'

'In truth?' said Mr Henry. 'Nice, nice – tell yu Mammy and Pappy good-night for me.' And Mr Henry moved on. There were other footsteps, each set filling us with excitement, and then with profound disappointment. Our spirits were flagging, and sleep was beginning to get the better of us too. Then our hopes rose again as we heard a whole shuffle of footsteps approaching. It might be two people coming down the road! I hoisted Toddan up again so that his eyes were even with the sill. In the darkness I could make out two figures. Toddan was hopping up and down with glee.

Then I heard singing and knew it was only Miss Terry taking – dragging – Mr Christopher home again, Mr Christopher being stone drunk and singing at the top of his voice 'Gimme piece o' yu dumplin Mae dou-dou.' We crouched down instinctively. Everybody on the street hauled their children inside when this particular procession came past on evenings, and many a youngster had had his tongue washed with household soap for launching into the refrain of 'Gimme piece o'yu dumplin Mae dou-dou', so that Miss Terry and Mr Christopher were a sinister and unaccountable mystery. When they had gone by I got up again, but Toddan did not move. Then his fat body rolled to one side – he was fast asleep.

Long after Toddan had been carted off to bed I stayed at the window, struggling to keep my eyes open. There were fewer people going past now so that I all but fell asleep between each set of footsteps. But I always revived to see if it was them, and if not to shout 'We gettin a baby!' to whoever it was.

◆

Then Papa was easing my head off the window-sill and there was a great agitation all around. People were coming into the house and Tantie was saying shshsh.

'*We will take the children,*' somebody said firmly, in a voice like high-heels and stockings. And an old voice was wailing: 'Poor lil infant, ohhh lam of Gord . . .' Papa was gathering me up and when he saw that I was awake said 'Hush' in a distracted way. His face was like a stranger's.

Ma Peters' wailing was disconcerting; the firm voice with high-heels and stockings was still saying '*We will take the children*' and Mr Lucifer was declaiming in aggressive tones: 'What the Lord give the Lord have every right to take-back . . .' Some quavery voices scraped themselves together into a slow singing, and then Toddan's shriek pierced the bedroom wall, and Papa, still carrying me, made a limping dash in that direction.

Toddan cried and cried and then rested and started up again. There were people in the house all night long and there was the smell of coffee and of rum. There was singing, now mournful, with a grumble of men's voices welling up under the shrill ones, now to the accompaniment of drumming on the table or bottle-

and-spoon. Tantie sat on our bed. Once the high-heels and stockings voice tock-tocked into the room and ignoring Tantie completely patted Toddan on the arm and said: 'Don't cry, darling, you're coming home with your Auntie tomorrow.' Toddan bit her hand. Tantie laughed a little. The voice drew herself up: 'Look at you, you aren't *fit*!' and stalked out of the room.

'Monkey can't see 'e own tail,' murmured Tantie to herself.

◆

The house was still full of people and there were flowers in thick bunches that didn't look like flowers at all but like a bristly covering for some sinister animal sleeping underneath; there was a shiny thing in a corner that I was afraid to look at and then an old woman took my hand and led me towards the corner and I grasped her hand tightly and shut my eyes and suddenly I was being lifted into the air and opening my eyes in alarm saw that I was passing over the shiny thing half-smothered by ugly, still stuck-together flowers and then I landed into the shaky arms of another old lady on the other side; and then they picked up Toddan and he screamed and kicked, so that they nearly dropped him with fright.

◆

It was the middle of the night, because Toddan and I had been to bed. He was a limp bundle curled over Papa's shoulder, his shoes dangling, and Mikey was carrying me. The air was a green smell. The night seemed to be blowing like soft wind somewhere out beyond the edges of our patch of light. Then Spottie and Puppie came rushing down towards us in a tangled knot which hurled itself at Tantie; darkness dropped over the

3

path and Tantie cursed them vehemently as she groped around on the ground for the torch.

I fell asleep again with Mikey sitting on the bed. Papa came on evenings and there was much talk of 'that woman' and 'that bitch' who wanted to get us. This filled me with alarm. Who wanted to 'get' us and how could they get us when Papa was there, and Tantie and Mikey, or were they too going to disappear? I fell asleep at night tightly clutching a bit of Toddan's night-clothes and with one toe touching Tantie.

Then Papa went to sea. I concluded that what he had gone to see was whether he could find Mammy and the baby.

2

Tantie's company was loud and hilarious and the intermittent squawk and flurry of mirth made me think of the fowl-run when something fell into the midst of the fat hens. Mr Gordon was always darting round with a wicked expression on his face, tearing up the fattest of the macommè's from their chairs to dance and they floundered up with much raucous protestation. The children scurried about giddily; sometimes we were coaxed inside to dance, sometimes to our delight the company spread over a whole weekend, like at Tantie's birthday. Then even Mikey was in a consistent good humour.

The trouble was only with the Uncles; Tantie upbraided Mikey for slouching through the drawingroom without even Good-evening-dog and Mikey insisted that he always said good-evening and Tantie said yu call that good-evenin a grunt down in yu belly? and Mikey said yu want mih kiss them? and Tantie

4

said who 'them', is Mr George I talkin about, I don' know who you mean by 'them' who is 'them'? And he took to slouching in through the back door instead. And the rampage when Leila went out the window and broke it was the night when Uncle Herman had leant back in his chair taking out a cigarette and said bigly to Mikey: 'Well, son – yu Nen been tellin me – yu in lil difficulty an t'ing – but do' bother – jobwise, the ol' Homey sure to fix yu up wit somet'ing – leave it to me.'

And Mikey who was only on his way through the drawing-room disappeared into his room all the same muttering shortly: 'Do' study me, br'ar.'

Tantie plunged into the room after him, and there was compressed hissing, pending the volcano in store for after Uncle Herman left. When Tantie was thwarted the neighbours for six houses on every side of us were generally aware of this fact.

'. . . yu t'ink blasted saga-clothes an' t'eater does grow on tree? An' before yu look to help-out yu mother an' she forty-nine chirren no yu prefer siddong on yu arse wid them long wu'tless youngmen down at that bridge . . .'

'Awright, man, I go jus' go down by mih mother an' say yu put me out . . .'

'Hear how yu talkin through yu arse again, I ever put yu out? An' go down by yu mother an where she go put yu? On top the roof? Under the house? An' yu ain' shame you reach a big long youngman an' she still dey ketchin she tail with the lil ol'-house falling-down on she head? . . .'

And as was not uncommon, Mikey in the long run left the house precipitately to the accompaniment of flying objects, on this occasion including Leila with the blood-red cheeks and the startled eyebrows who happened to be at hand. Mikey stood behind the protective shaddock tree as was his wont and told Tantie what was what.

The only Uncle we remembered with any distaste was Uncle

Nero. Whenever he arrived he would summon us, if we hadn't managed to hide, and stare at us fixedly for a long time, as if to penetrate us, then: 'Behavin good?'

'Yes, Uncle Nero,' we would squirm.

'Allyu doin what yu Tantie tell yu, or yu harden'?' with his hand on his belt. 'How they behavin', Rosa? Keep them straight, yu know, keep them straight! Awright allyu, go an find some work to do, quick sharp!'

One of them gave us a scooter for Christmas, which we quickly discarded again for the one Mikey made us with board and motor-car parts and which made that delicious grinding noise on the road; Mikey took the wheels off the bright shiny blue-and-red scooter to make us a box-cart.

Mikey made us a swing, too, on the low branch of the mango-vert tree, but there was jumbie living in the tree, he said, so that was why the swing broke down every few days.

Life was wonderful when he was out of a job, and in a good mood, which was less predictable. There were days when we would be as quiet as mice from morning till night, or kept out of his range altogether. But we would rather die than report to Tantie that he had delivered one of us a sound back-hand slap for vexing him. The rest of the time we were strutting in his shadow, off to raid the Estate or down to the Savannah to fly our kites that he made us; or it was the long, long walk with the sun all around and stinging and blurryness rising from the road and the smell of asphalt, and the road soft under your toes and the grass at the sides no cooler and just when it was getting too much we'd turn off the road and plunge between the bushes and down down the precipitous path to the water; and Mikey cruising around in the deep part with one lazy eye on us; and in between the stones busy little fishes with big heads; and boat-races with leaves and our leaves could never sail straight but spun crazily . . .

Often we went down with him to the steelband shed where Santa Clara Syncos practised, and sometimes he beat a second-pan. At the shed there was usually a fringe of children hanging about, and they let us shake the chac-chac; there were some little boys who were regular pan-men and who even got to beat a pan on the road at Carnival. The players felt about idly and aimlessly on their pans for a long spell until without one noticing the sounds had converged into order. So close to the band the bass-pans thudded through your belly, and the iron-section with the sounds crashing out from the touch of the tiny stick on the anonymous piece of engine entrails was your teeth clashing together in time with the beat. With boisterous relish we supplied the choruses that hugged and danced with the music or darted and threaded airily in and out of it.

Mikey took us down to the bridge from time to time, always reminding us in no uncertain terms before we set out of what would befall us at his hands if we breathed a word to Tantie for he wasn't having that settin'-hen takin a turn in his arse. There was nothing Tantie could do to break Mikey's association with the assortment down at the bridge, who were the cream of Santa Clara's unambitious, but as for taking us down there with him – we had a pretty good idea of what would take place if she were to find out.

The fellows mainly discussed last weekend's Tarzan picture or Western, or passed around the latest Danger Man comic book, or they discussed the horses if races were on; or they gave the floor to Manhatt'n.

Manhatt'n was an individual who at some obscure date had 'gone-away'. Some of the boys said he'd only been to Curaçao where he'd got a job for a few months; one section of opinion had it that he'd merely worked down on the Base for a few weeks. Manhatt'n himself gave it out that he'd been up State-side, fellers, up Amurraca-side – for he always spoke with his mouth screwed to one side and all the words coming out of his nose. When the fellows were in a tolerant mood they would let Manhatt'n tell of his encounter with the sheriff in Dodge City and how he outdrew him; or of the blonde chick in Manhattan who wouldn't leave him alone, kept coming to his apartment when there was this red-head thing he was working at (Martinis, yer know, and a lil'cavriar on the side). And when the fellows screamed with laughter Manhatt'n looked imbecilically happy. But when one day someone maliciously murmured 'Crick-crack!' at the end of one of these accounts in perfect Western drawl, Manhatt'n in his rage forgot to screw his mouth to one side before starting to speak.

'Crick-crack yu mother! Is true whe ah tell yu – yu only blasted jealous it ain' you! Crick-crack? Ah go crick-crack yu stones gi' yu!'

Manhatt'n was seen rather less at the bridge after that, and furthermore the fellows now thought nothing of addressing him as Fresh-water, the name they had formerly used only behind his back.

Women going past walked a gauntlet of commentary on their anatomy and deportment. And for Mrs Hinds in particular they had no mercy. Like any proper lady (it seemed to me) she had a high, stiff bottom and spectacles and stockings.

'Mind, Mis' Hinds, the bottom fallin!' a disembodied voice would offer.

'Mind the bus'es and them, too, Mis' Hinds, yu might over-balance with all that weight in front there,' in a sing-song lady-voice.

'How she go overbalance,' contested another with irritation, 'that is what the bottom there for! Yu never hear 'bout ballast or what?'

And Mrs Hinds would turn and lecture them with the most careful enunciation on the moral evils of vagabondage, a lecture which the boys punctuated copiously with dramatic sighs of 'Oh yes, Lord!' and 'True-spoke, sister, Amen!' and 'Glory, glory be!'

There was one memorable time when Mikey took us along to the bridge. When we arrived a discussion was in full swing. Lamp-post was enthusing.

'Western in yu arse, boy, Western in yu arse!' and Joe was recreating the climax with a lively pantomime: ''ey boy, forty-million o'them against the star-boy and the rest o'them ridin comin and then he bullets run-out . . .'

'An' then the other guys reach, an' then, ol'-man, then yu jus' see Red-Indian fallin-dong all over the place – ba-da-da-da-da – pretty, boy, pretty!' mused Krishna.

Then Marina came along and when she had passed by (she always strutted by with her head in the air, but slowly, and with a peculiar smile on her face) they were talking idly, laughing boisterouly from time to time and it was when a young man going by the appellation Audie-Murphy (there were also a Rock-Hudson and a Gary-Cooper in the company) said to Mikey something that sounded like 'Wha 'bout yu Nennen, boy, ask she if I can't pass in by she too, nuh?' that it all began. Mikey was suddenly on top of Audie-Murphy and they were rolling all over the ground and pounding each other and threshing about with their arms and legs and dust was flying and the others were crowding round eagerly.

We watched, stupefied, for what seemed hours; for suddenly it was dark and suddenly we were being torn up from the ground by firm hands, propped on the bars of two bicycles and propelled down the road with much metallic creaking and clanking. Then we were abruptly deposited at our front gate and Basdeo and Tall-Boy jangled off at great speed.

We ran up the path as fast as our legs could carry us. Tantie had come home and excitedly we delivered our account of the baffling affair.

It was when Tantie's features began to knot themselves hard together that I remembered with a plunge of dismay that we should never tell her that we had been down at the bridge. But it was too late. We had already told the whole story, which was brief enough. I waited for the rampage to begin. But Tantie stood with her forehead creased as if she were thinking of something else.

'What it is the boy tell Mikey?' she asked vacantly.

We told her again. Still nothing happened but it could only mean that she was saving up the rampage for when Mikey came home. She moved about the house in silence, setting the table, going to the window every few minutes and peering up the dark road.

I sat frozen. I wanted to go to bed and be asleep with the pillow over my head when Mikey came home. But I could not go to bed and leave Mikey to face a storm of our making. So I waited miserably. And the cocoa was getting cold and everybody was hungry – Mikey was surely coming home to his execution this time.

When we heard his step in the gallery my heart and my stomach exchanged places. Mikey slouched in. His jersey was of an indefinable colour and the hem of it half torn loose was draping his hips drunkenly like a gunbelt. His hair and face looked as if they had been powdered. And the expression on his face told that he would willingly batter the rest of us into the earth if we looked at him too hard.

'Water in the bedroom, Mikey,' was all she said. And then she hurried into the kitchen to heat up the cocoa. And when the sound of water could no longer be heard in Mikey's room she called to him in what seemed to me a *reverent* voice: 'The tea on the table, Mikey.'

'Do' wan' no damn tea, man,' came a surly voice from out of the darkness. Now, I thought, now we're going to get it. First of all: yu t'ink this is a blasted boardin'-house yu t'ink yu is the Governor or who yu ain' put no servant here yu know . . . and then she would work round, in ample time, to the bridge and us.

But Tantie spread some slices of bread alarmingly thickly with butter, heaped some of the smoke'-herring onto a plate with the bread, went to the cabinet and took out a large mug that was Grampa's which she filled up with cocoa and bore the lot *reverently* into the hostile darkness of Mikey's room.

When she came out again I was still staring at the door.

'Eat!' she snapped, startling me.

3

The threat that we had come to designate compendiously as 'The Bitch' hovered over every day of our lives. Auntie Beatrice started by writing a succession of letters to Tantie and upon the receipt of each letter Tantie would rage for about an hour. We had clear instructions what to do if The Bitch turned up while neither Tantie nor Mikey was there – we were to run over to Neighb' Ramlaal-Wife and stay there; and if Neighb' Ramlaal-Wife wasn't there we were to go to Neighb' Doris; or to Tan' Mavis, or down to Marva-Mother. Half the street was involved in the barricade against The Bitch.

And so Auntie Beatrice, who was only a blurred Distant Lady in our memory, grew horns and a djablesse-face and a thousand attributes of female terrifyingness, with the result that we did not scamper off in terror and panic when one peaceful afternoon as we were sitting on the front step with me playing teacher to a bored and unimpressed class consisting of Toddan and Doolarie, a car drew up and a lady with a benignant smile alighted. She descended upon us and smothered us with kissing and clouds of a dull perfume that issued out from her clothes. Doolarie withdrew to a cautious distance. Then our visitor opened her handbag and took out some sweets; Doolarie edged forward again, tentatively. After she had filled our hands with sweets she extended her arm and held one out to Doolarie, saying, a note of severeness which we did not understand having crept into her voice: 'Here, child, and go home, eh? You' Ma mus' be looking for you.'

Doolarie's sweet disappeared into her mouth and she stayed. Then Auntie Beatrice turned her beam onto us again: 'Your Auntie is not at home, is she?'

'No,' we chorused.

'And the boy?'

'He gone to work.'

'Well how would you like to go for a nice drive in your Uncle Norman's car?'

I was inclined to deliberate over the matter, but since Toddan accepted with enthusiasm I reflected with the sageness of the older that a problem of greater magnitude would be how to quiet him down if we didn't go.

As we rose to go Toddan in his joy gallantly took the hand of our tiny playmate: 'Tum, Doolayie,' and started to lead her down towards the car. Auntie Beatrice separated them firmly and again bade Doolarie go home. Again she only withdrew a few feet and stood staring, wide-eyed and expressionless, as we went down the path with our unexpected benefactor.

At the wheel of the car there sat a bored-looking man staring idly ahead of him. He turned slightly and glanced at us as we approached, then continued to stare at nothing in particular. As Auntie Beatrice piled us into the back seat she said to him with irritation: 'You see how she has these coolie children running about with them?' The man grunted.

As we drove Auntie Beatrice talked non-stop. Did that woman leave us there alone in the day-time and did she beat us and then what about all those men did we like all those men coming and then what about when she got drunk – and this punctuated by stops along the way to buy ice-cream and roast-corn and by asides to Uncle Norman who either grunted or didn't bother. We replied to her prodding in between mouthfuls of roast-corn and ice-cream and sweets, so much that by the time the car drew up at our gate again the arrangement was that Toddan and I were going to press and harrass Tantie to let us come and spend the August vacation with Bernadette and Carol and Jessica and Auntie Beatrice and Uncle Norman.

There was a sizeable gathering in our front yard and I wondered what had happened. I could make out Tan Mavis and Georgina and Moonie and Ma-Philippa. When the car stopped Toddan jumped out and ran excitedly up the path.

'Tantie! Tantie! We went for a dwive! We went for a dwive! an' we get . . .'

Tantie's figure detached itself from the knot and precipitated itself frantically down the path; she snatched Toddan up and hauled me to her side in the same savage movement. Then she stood her ground and faced the car. Toddan had dried up, subdued by Tantie's agitation, and I was suffering something akin to the after-effects of a bucket of cold water poured over my head.

Auntie Beatrice and Uncle Norman stayed in the parked car; when Tantie had found her voice again what she ain' tell that bitch is what she forget. Or didn't have the time: after they had heard enough of Tantie's mind the car jerked off.

◆

13

Tantie raged all evening. An' she had a mind not to give us anything to eat because allyu belly must be done full wid that bitch ice-cream and sweetie. She raged and rampaged with no indication of subsiding, so that Mikey finally got up and left the house with a loud cheups; she called down curses on his departing figure and then returned to Auntie Beatrice and our escapade. She reiterated for the hundredth time what could have happened to us: we had jus' nearly get we arse kidnap'! And then the thought of it became uncontainable; she flew at me and battered me with the dishcloth she had in her hand, hitting out in furious relief.

Then she set the table, almost on tip-toe.

4

The very next day we were being hustled off to Ma, away away up in Pointe d'Espoir, with Toddan falling asleep on Mikey's lap as usual and Mikey having to climb the track with him over one shoulder and the suitcase in the other hand. When we came back it would be time for me to go to school, and Toddan they could simply lose among Neighb' Ramlaal-Wife's own when there was no one at home.

The August holidays had already begun, so that all the multitude was there. Our grandmother was a strong, bony woman who did not smile unnecessarily, her lower jaw set forward at an angle that did not brook opposition or argument. She did not use up too many words at a time either, except when she sat on the step with us teeming around her, when there was a moon, and told us 'nancy-stories. If the night was too dark or if it was raining there was no story-telling – it was inconceivable to her that one should sit inside a house and tell 'nancy-stories. At full moon there was a bonus and then we would light a black-sage fire for the mosquitoes and sand-flies and the smoke smelt like contented drowsiness. And when at the end of the story she said 'Crick crack?' our voices clambered over one another in the gleeful haste to chorus back in what ended on an untidy shrieking crescendo:

> Monkey break 'e back
> On a rotten pommerac!

And there was no murmur of protest when she ordered with finality: 'That is enough. Find allyu bed.'

On most afternoons we descended to the beach in a great band, Ma saluting houses on the way:

'Oo-oo Ma-Henrietta!'

'Oo-oo!' a voice would answer from the depths of the house or from somewhere in the backyard.

'Is me an' mih gran's passin'.'

'Right, Ma-Josephine!'

Ma brought with her a wooden box and a stick. While we splashed about in the water she sat immobile and straight-backed on her box, her hands resting together on the stick which she held upright in front of her. When someone started to venture too far out she rapped sharply on the box with the stick. And when it was time to go she rapped again: 'Awright. Come-out that water now!'

Then we walked along the sand, straggled and zig-zagged and played along the sand, to where they drew the nets in, and we 'helped' in this latter operation, fastening ourselves like a swarm of bees to the end of the rope and adding as much to the total effort as would a swarm of bees bunched at the end of the thick hauling-rope. Afterwards we swooped down and collected the

15

tiny fishes that they left on the beach, and Ma let us roast these in the fire at home.

Ma's land was to us an enchanted country, dipping into valley after valley, hills thickly covered with every conceivable kind of foliage, cool green darknesses, sudden little streams that must surely have been squabbling past in the days when Brar Anancy and Brar Leopard and all the others roamed the earth outsmarting each other. And every now and then we would lose sight of the sea and then it would come into sight again down between trees when you least expected to see it, and always, it seemed, in a different direction; that was frightening too. We went out with Ma to pick fruit, she armed with a cutlass with which she hacked away thick vines and annihilated whole bushes in one swing. We returned with our baskets full of oranges, mangoes, chennettes, Ma bent under a bunch of plantains that was more than half her size.

Ma had a spot in the market on Sunday mornings, and she spent a great part of the week stewing cashews, pommes-cythères, cerises, making guava-cheese and guava jelly, sugar-cake, nut-cake, bennay-balls, toolum, shaddock-peel candy, chilibibi . . . On these days we hung slyly about the kitchen, if only to feed on the smells; we were never afforded the opportunity of gorging ourselves – we partook of these delicacies when Ma saw fit, and not when we desired. She was full of maxims for our edification, of which the most baffling and maddening was:

> Who ask
> don't get
> Who don't ask
> don't want
> Who don't want
> don't get
> Who don't get
> don't care.

For her one of the cardinal sins of childhood was gluttony: 'Stuff yu guts today an' eat the stones of the wilderness tomorrow.' (Ma's sayings often began on a note of familiarity only to rise into an impressive incomprehensibility, or vice versa, as in 'Them that walketh in the paths of corruption will live to ketch dey arse.')

She was equal to all the vagaries of childhood. Nothing took her by surprise – she never rampaged, her initial reaction was always a knowing 'Hm'. Not that one permitted oneself the maximum of vagaries in Ma's house – her eye was too sharp and her hand too quick. But there were the odd times that somebody thought she wasn't looking. Sometimes there would be a chase, exciting but brief, when the culprit was hauled back panting to face the music in front of us all. Sometimes he was merely set free again, since he was already frightened to death and would certainly never try that one again.

Just as there were enough of us to play Hoop and Rescue and every conceivable game, so there were enough of us for the occasional outbreak of miniature gang-warfare. We sat for hours under the house in two camps proffering hearty insults. The division usually fell between those who were kept by Ma and those of us who didn't really live there. Ma's children were the 'bush-monkeys' and 'country-bookies' and they in turn made it known to us how deep was their longing for the day when we would all depart so they could have their house and their yard and their land to themselves again. This stung deep for though we knew beyond doubt that it was equally our house and yard and land yet it was those fiends who lived in the house all year round and played in the yard and went on expeditions into the land with Ma when we were not there. If hostilities lasted till a mealtime, then we placed ourselves on opposite sides of the table and eyed each other with contempt. And if they lasted until night-time, then going to bed was an uncomfortable affair, for it took rather longer to fall asleep when every muscle of your body and every inch of your concentration was taut with the effort of not touching your neighbour. But we the vacation batch always had our revenge when it was time to go home and our big-people had come to fetch us and we were all dressed up for the trip home and being fussed over – Ma's children looked a little envious then.

Ma awoke every morning with a groan quickly routed by a brief loud cheups. She rose at a nameless hour and in my half-sleep I saw a mountain shaking off mist in one mighty shudder and the mist falling away in little drops of cloud. The cheups with which Ma greeted the day expressed her essential attitude before the whole of existence – what yu mus' beat-up yuself for? In the face of the distasteful and unavoidable, the unexpected and irreversible, all that Ma could not crush or confound with a barked word or surmount with her lioness strength, she reacted to with a cheups, more or less loud, more or less long. Thus she sucked her teeth loudly and without further comment when the iron pot full of rice spitefully tipped itself over into the fire; when the sun took to playing monkey-wedding with the rain the moment she had put the final clothes-peg to her miles of washing strung from the breadfruit tree to the zaboca tree, from the zaboca tree to the house-post and from the house-post to the chicken-run post, Ma sucked her teeth and turned her back.

And there were the days of real rain. We could see it coming, down across the water, a dark ceiling letting down slow grey streamers into the horizon (that was God pee-peeing into his posie) and then it would be pounding the earth like a thousand horses coming at us through the trees. It was frightening and exciting. A sudden greyness had descended upon everything and we had seconds in which to race about the yard like mad-ants helping Ma to place her assortment of barrels and buckets in

18

places where they would catch the water. And all the time the rain pounding nearer, racing to catch us. When the first messenger spray hit us there was pandemonium – we stampeded into the house, some squealing with a contagious excitement. We ran round shutting the windows, pulling out buckets and basins to place under the leaks, still squealing and colliding with each other. As the windows were closed one by one a cosy darkness crept in, and we felt as if our numbers were growing. We all collected into one room. Sometimes we piled onto the big-bed and made a tent of the coverlets, tying them to the four posts of the bed. Under the tent the commotion was sustained, rising to squealing pitch at every flash of lightning and crack of thunder, or every time the tent collapsed about us, or when a lath fell so that a part of the bed caved in under some of us; or when someone chose this situation of inescapable intimacy to emit an anonymous but very self-assertive poops. It was impossible to detect the owner, and chaos ensued while every man accused his immediate neighbour. In the end we had to count the culprit out by means of Ink-Pink-Mamma-Stink, and the man thus denounced was emitted bodily amidst a new burst of commotion.

Meanwhile Ma bustled about the house – we knew that she was just as excited as we were, barricaded into the darkened house with the rain drumming on the galvanize and surrounding us with heavy purring like a huge mother-cat. Ma seemed to be finding things to do so as not to yield to the temptation to come and crawl under the sheets and play tent with us. Then she came in with a big plate of sugar-cake and guava-cheese, and pretended to be scandalized at the way we were treating the bedclothes.

And when the rain had stopped we dressed up in Grampa's old jackets and went out with Ma to look at the river. This was like a ritual following upon the rain – she had to go and see the

19

river. We walked behind her squelching joyously in the new puddles and mud. The air smelt brown and green, like when the earth was being made. From a long way off the river was calling to us through the trees, in one continuous groan, so that when we finally came to it, wet and splashed from the puddles and from the bushes we had brushed against, it was as though we had been straining along in it the whole time. Ma stopped abruptly and spread out both her arms to stop us, as though it were likely that we would keep on walking right into the fast ochre water. We counted how many trees it had risen past on the bank. If the river came down every week Ma's rapture would be quite as new.

'Eh!' she exclaimed, and then fell back into her trance. Then a little later on 'Eh!' shaking her head from side to side, 'Well yes, well yes!' We stood around her in an unlikely silence like spattered acolytes in our jumble-sale clothes, in the bright air hanging out crisp and taut to dry, and the river ploughing off with the dirt and everything drenched and bowing and satisfied and resting before the world started up again from the beginning.

◆

We roamed the yard and swarmed down to the water and played hoop around the breadfruit tree as if we would always be wiry-limbed children whose darting about the sun would capture like amber and fix into eternity. Although Ma exclaimed upon our arrival each year at how big we'd got, yet all the holidays at Pointe d'Espoir were one August month, especially in the middle part of the day when everything seemed to set in the still, hanging brightness – our games and squabbling; the hens with their heads down scratching about the yard; the agreeableness of sitting clamped between Ma's knees having one's hair plaited. The cream air in the middle part of the day was like Time staring at itself in a mirror, the two faces locked dreamily in an eternal gaze.

I was Ma's own-own bold-face Tee, harden' as the Devil's shit but that is yu great great grandmother, that is she, t'ank Gord. Sometimes when the others were not about she would accost me suddenly: 'An who is Ma sugar-cake?'

'Tee!'

'An who is Ma dumplin'?'

'Tee!'

And all at once she put on an expression of mock-displeasure and snapped at me gruffly: 'Who tell yu that?'

'Ma tell mih!'

'Well Ma is a liard ol'-fool'; and she thrust a hunk of guava-cheese at me.

Ma said that I was her grandmother come back again. She said her grandmother was a tall straight proud woman who lived to an old old age and her eyes were still bright like water and her back straight like bamboo, for all the heavy-load she had carried on her head all her life. The People gave her the name Euphemia or Euph-something, but when they called her that she used to toss her head like a horse and refuse to answer so they'd had to give up in the end and call her by her true-true name.

Then Ma creased her forehead and closed her eyes and rubbed her temples and if anyone spoke she waved her hand with irritation. She sat like this for a long time. Then she would shake her head sorrowfully. She couldn't remember her grandmother's true-true name. But Tee was growing into her grandmother again, her spirit was in me. They'd never bent down her spirit and she would come back and come back and come back; if only she could live to see Tee grow into her tall proud straight grandmother.

5

I looked forward to school. I looked forward to the day when I could pass my hand swiftly from side to side on a blank piece of paper leaving meaningful marks in its wake; to staring nonchalantly into a book until I turned over the page, a gesture pregnant with importance for it indicated that one had not merely been staring, but that that most esoteric of processes had been taking place whereby the paper had yielded up something or other as a result of having been stared at.

At the next re-opening Tantie took me to school, so early in the morning it was still a little dark. But when we got to the school there was already a restless army of women outside the closed gate with children squashed among them, children beginning to send up a peevish protest. The women seemed to be directing a great deal of temper at an unconcerned man sitting on a box inside the schoolyard reading a newspaper. Never once did he throw a glance in our direction, for all the abuse and gesticulation of the women; he sat immobile, and every time he made the slightest movement the crowd surged forward irresistibly, arriving no further than crushing each other's feet and grinding tempers thinner.

After an age, with the sun's heat and the crowd growing, a voice called to the watchman from inside the building; he nodded, folded up his newspaper with exaggerated thoroughness, laid it aside and set out towards the gate at a resentful pace.

At the gate he faced the women and delivered a brief, sullen speech: 'Mind how allyu come-in this gate. If allyu push, ah closin it back.'

'Mr Oliver, shut yu face an' open the damn gate,' was one of the replies he received.

We charged. Or the women charged and we children tumbled in among them. We were making for a door.

Suddenly there was no further progress to be made – we were being flattened into each other's backs and standing on the same spot; for those at the very front had filled up the office and the greater part of the throng was still outside.

So we stood for another age, with people minus their charges squeezing their way back out through the tightly-pressed company who were not altogether inclined to assist them by giving way. As more and more people left we were edging closer and closer to the door; until the rumour made its way out to us that there was no more room in ABC class. Immediately people with older children began to struggle forward, to the irritation of those with ABC candidates, who remarked loudly at their lack of manners in pushing and jostling.

When that movement was complete there still remained a sizeable crowd of people who apparently had no intention of giving ground. The watchman appeared from nowhere, ostensibly transporting a bucket of something from one point to another, but looking as though this were a moment he had waited for with keen relish. As he slouched past us he muttered: 'Why allyu do' go-home, yu can't understan' or what, no room is no room!' and was instructed by a pugnacious voice to go an' scratch his arse.

Then Mr Thomas made his way with difficulty through the crowd adamantly installed inside his office and who seemed to think he was attempting escape; he stood in our midst, closely hemmed in, and pleaded with us distraughtly to go away. When nobody budged he rubbed his temples and threw up his hands in frustration:

'Look, what allyu want me to do, put allyu children to

siddong on one-another head? I tell yu I ain' have no more room in ABC – try the RC school, put them by Mis' Hinds, send them up Coriaca school, I do' care what allyu do jus' carry them 'way and yu could bring them back when they pass ABC!'

When a few people at the edge of the crowd began to move off rather precipitately we needed no further persuasion. With one accord we surged out of the schoolyard, and soon we were but the hairsbreadth of civilization away from pushing each other over and running over the fallen. It was nevertheless a race, if a slightly shamefaced race, down the road and across the Savannah to the RC school. Many of Tantie's cronies were in the hustling company – none acknowledged the other.

Then we were before the gate of the RC school. But the gate was shut and there was a piece of cardboard with letters on it that must have conveyed the fact that there was no more room. Behind the gate there was a plump nun with red cheeks and glasses, her hands together as if she was praying, her head cocked on one side and a regretful smile on her face; I thought too that her eyes were shut, only it might have been her glasses. And she was swaying diagonally, presumably also with regret.

The race slackened, the women relaxed into cronies again, thrown back in a heap together, their rivalry abruptly ampu-tated. They gathered in a chattering knot which dwindled after a while as they went off with their children, still delivering their piece o' mind in loud tones. The nun swayed on and smiled regretfully, as if she had been wound up and placed at the gate to do so.

So Tantie had to take me down to Mrs Hinds, a horrible capitulation, for she'd always sworn she'd never send a dog of hers there, that woman was a mauvais'-langue horse-face maco with nothing to do but mind people's business. We marched down to Mrs Hinds, Tantie muttering all the way her disap-proval and disgust blasted government wouldn' build school for the chirren what the blasted government there for but to build school for the chirren now look my cross I have to put the chile by these shifters all they know is to run behind the Reveren' arse an' he wife an' smell every fart they blow when it was black-arse Reverend Joseph God res' he soul they used to find their arse to Hell up in Coriaca Church on a Sunday morning me I would shit on all o' them jus' you remember you going there to learn *book* do' let them put no blasted shit in yu head.

As we walked up the concrete steps a disorderly chanting straggled out to us from behind a half-open door.

Mrs Hinds was sitting with a piece of embroidery. The children were placed around two tables, the boys at one and the girls at the other. Tantie and Mrs Hinds had a brief discussion, Mrs Hinds turgid with dignity, Tantie akimbo and insolent.

I was given a place among the chanting which went on and on and became more and more disorderly as more and more voices either dropped out, chanted at half a second's interval after the confident voices or simply became a drone keeping in time with the rhythm. Mrs Hinds embroidered. After some time, at around the seven-times table it must have been, there were only about four tenuous voices articulating anything, the rest were a rhythmic drone. Then even the drone slackened; and Mrs Hinds looked up from her embroidery with an inquisitive expression on her face, whereupon the drone immediately quick-ened again. When the noise came to a complete halt Mrs Hinds said 'All right, recess,' and I nearly fell off my end of the bench as all my colleagues rose abruptly. Everybody pushed towards the door in a horrible noise and confusion; a sharp interjection from Mrs Hinds and they stood stock still: 'Orderly, orderly, file out orderly!'

I remained in my place. 'Recess, darling, you don't want to go out and play?' Go out and play indeed, when I had come to this place to read and write and all the other mysteries one performed at school! Go out and play I would indeed not. This whole enterprise known as school was proving a trifle unexpected in more than one of its aspects.

Mrs Hinds went out and after a while a bell rang and the children tumbled in again. Mr Hinds came in through another door and stood at the head of the boys' table wagging a ruler and looking stern, waiting for them to settle down. He had a greying swirly moustache and wore a brown suit on the jacket of which there was some kind of a badge in the shape of a shield, and a tie that had gold and blue stripes; he frequently flapped his jacket and mopped his head but however hot it became never did it seem to occur to Mr Hinds to remove his jacket.

Everyone knew that Mr Hinds had been up in England in his young-days, that was why he talked in that way, that he had fought in the war and that he had nearly got to be a lawyer but instead he had come back to be the Headmaster of Coriaca EC.

High on the wall behind Mr Hinds hung a large framed portrait of Churchill. It was Mr Hinds' daily endeavour to bring the boys to a state of reverence towards this portrait; when they became rowdy he would still them into shame at their unworthy behaviour in the very sight of the greatest Englishman who ever lived etc, or he would still them into incomprehension because in his angry rhetorical transports he soared into a vocabulary that fell like gibberish on the ear. But all his own outraged respect, all his resounding tales of the war and the glorious victories for some reason never did infect us with the required awe – for us the personage on the wall was and remained simply Crapaud-Face.

To Mrs Hinds' noble bottom I have already referred. When she stood she always had her arm resting on top of it or brushing swiftly over it as if to see whether it was still there, or perhaps to smooth it out of existence.

But Mrs Hinds didn't do too much standing. She sat in her

chair with a piece of embroidery or other sewing and from time to time addressed someone without raising her head in a slow commanding voice that grated effortlessly over the bedlam. Often her mother came tottering and groping into the room and arranged herself laboriously onto a chair. She had a cloth around her head with grey plaits sticking out all around from under it, and she was known to us as The Ol'-Lady. Conversation between Mrs Hinds and The Ol'Lady was a slow business for Mrs Hinds had to repeat every other word as The Ol'-Lady's hearing wasn't too good, and her voice was like a foreign radio station, fading out and in and cracking, and all the *s*'s fizzing out through the spaces between what teeth she had.

On my first day at school Mrs Hinds called to me to come to her with my slate. Across the top of it she made a row of identical creatures and handed slate and pencil back to me saying: 'Here, make A for Apple,' and took up her embroidery again. I went back to my place and after a few moments of bewilderment followed my neighbour's example in filling up the whole slate with things of the approximate shape of those made by Mrs Hinds.

Everybody else was scraping away at their slates, and occasionally someone effaced their hieroglyphics with a liberal wash of water (or spit) and then waved their slate about in the air singing:

> Jumbie Jumbie dry mih slate
> I'll give yu a penny toba-cco

and often slates tended to be waved smack into neighbours' faces, which tended to generate loud strife. Everybody seemed to know what they were about, everybody seemed to be in the middle of something.

My reading career also began with A for Apple, the exotic fruit that made its brief and stingy appearance at Christmastime, and pursued through my Caribbean Reader Primer One the fortunes and circumstances of two English children known as Jim and Jill, or it might have been Tim and Mary.

At about twelve o'clock we sang grace, 'Hands together, eyes shut!' and anyone caught with so much as one eye half-open receiving a sound slap. Then we scampered out, with admonitions from Mrs Hinds to 'Go straight home, don't dilly-dally on the way!'

On afternoons the tempo was slow. Lunch was still heavy in our bellies, the sun which had battered down at us on the way back to school was still outside besieging the walls, cooking the air inside the schoolroom, and everyone felt most like sleeping. So we stood and counted in unison to a hundred, or recited nursery rhymes about Little Boy Blue (what, in all creation, was a 'haystack'?) and about Little Miss Muffet who for some unaccountable reason sat eating her curls away.

Or under Mr Hinds' direction we would recite Children of the Empire Ye are Brothers All, or sing God Save the King and Land of Hope and Glory. This with many angry interruptions, Mr Hinds stamping and shouting and making us begin all over again and threatening to make us go and stand in the sun and sing even as in the depths of adversity his regiment had stood in biting cold and sung songs of patriotism and the snow had rung with the strains of God save the King; because we were slouching and not standing properly at attention – 'Not an eyelid must bat not a finger must twitch when we honour the Mother Country.' Mr Hinds was inordinately pleased with this morsel of his own composing which to his mind must have been worthy of 'Not a drum was heard, not a funeral note/As his corpse to the rampart we hurried . . .'

After recess we would settle down to another session of scraping, chattering among ourselves while some unfortunate stood unenviably close to Mr Hinds and stuttered out his reading-lesson about Tim and Jim who did a jig on the mat for a fig. Mrs Hinds sat with her needlework and if her mother was there chatting with her. They discussed the state of affairs in the household of such and such a child whose family was doomed to destruction because the father drank and the mother never sent the children to church. They discussed the pernicious 'Save-soul' Sunday-school to which so many Santa Clara children went – those people the way they carry on inside that place sometimes passing you would think they were singing calypsoes all the Reverend can warn these ignorant people not to send their children there for it's just like sending them to Baptist or Shango.

Every Sunday afternoon Tantie dressed Toddan and me and sent us to the Pentecost Sunday-school in preference to that of the Anglican church. Tantie never went near any kind of church herself, but there was no discussion as to our attendance, we went and that was that. It was just as though grown-ups sent us to see whether we could make better sense of it than they had been able to themselves.

Mrs Hinds naturally did what she could towards our redemption. For the day began and ended with the intoning of the sounds which we could perform without a fault while our thoughts drifted elsewhere behind our tightly-shut eyes:

> Our father (*which was plain enough*)
> witchartin
> heavn
> *HALLE*
> owèdbethyname
> *THY*
> kingdumkum
> *THY*
> willbedunnunnert
> azitizinevn . . .

When we had got to the end of that there was still the long and rather more devious path of Ibelieveingoderfathalmitie. Then we sang either

> We are but little children weak
> Nor born in any high estate –

which was of course The Estate – but who would want to be born up in there? Or else the other sweet and opaque one:

> Gen Terjesus me kan mile
> Loo kupon thy little chile
> Pi teemy simpliss City
> Suh fumee to come to thee

From the conversation of Mrs Hinds and The Ol'-Lady I gathered to my puzzlement that Toddan and I (glances in my direction fraught with concern) were being 'dragged-up', and – how desirable a fate (glances of envious awe and admiration) – that our Daddy was 'Up-There' and was surely going to send for us. So one day I asked Tantie what they meant.

My puzzlement remained because the next thing I knew Tantie was battling and struggling to get past Mikey who was barring the front door and saying do' bother Nennen do' bother with the ol'-bitch and Tantie was shouting and out of breath and shouting that she was going down and spit on that bitch so help mih Gord and Mikey said do' bother Nen yu will only get the child putout man wait till she leave there then you an'me will go and spit on the bitch and Tantie was panting and shouting get outa mih way boy. In the end Mikey had to help her back into the house and put her into a chair where she sat fanning herself while he went to fetch a cup of water. On his way to the kitchen he hissed at me fiercely under his breath: 'Now yu will know to keep yu tail shut an' do' come-home with everything yu hear them two dotish ol'-witch say!'

♦

One indolent afternoon we were sitting scraping on our slates and chattering and Mrs Hinds was sewing and raising her voice in order to penetrate to The Ol'-Lady; Mr Hinds was taking up the reading lesson of an individual known as Duncey-Joseph. It was Duncey-Joseph who had one day stalled for five minutes at g-r-a-p-e-s until, instructed in a roar from Mr Hinds to 'Look at the picture and say what you see!' had looked at the picture, lit up with sudden triumph and announced: 'G-r-a-p-e-s – chennette!'

Duncey-Joseph was stalling and stuttering and Mr Hinds was bellowing, now at him (right into his ear so that Duncey seemed to start several inches upwards) now at the rest of us: 'Silence! You nincompoops!' at which a kind of frightened hush would ensue, pregnant however with suppressed giggling, for Mr Hinds' word 'nincompoops' which we never heard elsewhere always seemed to us the height of incongruity, issuing as it did from the mouth of one who, we were certain, never committed the lapse of etiquette known to us by its onomatopoeic final syllable.

After the hush the bedlam would reinstate itself and swell to its former volume, with scraping and chattering and Jumbie Jumbie dry mih slate and Mrs Hinds shouting a word to her mother. And Duncey-Joseph stalled and stuttered and Mr Hinds bellowed and wiped his forehead and flapped his jacket. There were two sugar-bees trapped in the room, now zooming about our heads, now bashing themselves against a windowpane, their buzzing becoming more and more enraged.

Suddenly there was a sharp crack and Duncey-Joseph's high-pitched wail. Our din stopped abruptly. Alarm seized us, for Mr Hinds' ruler was rarely satisfied with one victim at a time.

'Damn you! Damn you! You confounded nincompoop!' He flung Duncey's book across the room to where it hit the wall and fell in an undignified heap on the floor. No one had the faintest inclination to giggle at Mr Hinds' terminology. 'You nincompoops!' thundered Mr Hinds, his ire spreading over us all as we fully expected it would. 'Go home all of you, go home and never come back here! You'll never get anywhere, you'll never better yourselves, you'll never be anything but – ' Mr Hinds choked with anger – '*piccaninnies*! Here I stand, trying to teach you to read and write the English language, trying to teach confounded *piccaninnies* to read and write, I – ' his voice rose and rose and he leaned further and further over the table so that the boys nearest him were paralysed into an uncomfortable slanting position – 'I who have sat on the benches of the Inns of Court!' He was banging his ruler on the table. 'I who have marched to glory side by side with His Majesty's bravest men – I don't have to stand here and busy myself with – with – ' his thundering became a mighty hiss: 'with *little black nincompoops*!' He flung the ruler down and hurried out, vehemently mopping his forehead and flapping his jacket.

A thick stillness remained. The Ol'-Lady sat tense, frowning with incomprehension, still straining forward as if an explanation was yet to come which would clear up her perplexity. When only the silence continued, growing taut with our sense of something horribly amiss having taken place, quite beyond the ordinary run of Mr Hinds' rampages, she groped after Mrs Hinds: 'Elda! Elda! What happen? What happen?' Mrs Hinds looked stricken; she was staring out of the door through which her husband had precipitated himself, and the voice of The Ol'-Lady seemed to jerk her back into a place where she would much rather not be. She dismissed us, hurriedly and with her

32

composure in a state of disarray that we never saw before and never since.

◆

Various kindly and elderly folk had long since assured me that my mother had gone to Glory. And now at school I had come to learn that Glory and The Mother Country and Up-There and Over-There had all one and the same geographical location. It made perfect sense that the place where my mother had gone, Glory, should also be known as The Mother Country. And then there was 'Land of Hope and Glory/Mother of the Free . . .'

Every Sunday at Sunday-school we were given a little card with a picture and a Bible verse – pictures of children with yellow hair standing around Jesus in fields of sickly flowers and with yellow rays emanating stiffly from all these personages, or the children with yellow hair kneeling with their hands clasped and their faces upturned towards some kind of sun that had one fat ray coming down at them. Thus it was that I had a pretty good idea of what kind of a place Glory must be, and of what happened to you there; for also at Sunday-school we sang:

> Till I cross the wide, wide water, Lord
> My <u>black</u> sin washèd from me,
> Till I come to Glory Glory, Lord
> And cleansèd stand beside Thee,
> <u>White</u> and shining stand beside Thee, Lord,
> Among Thy blessèd children . . .

[handwritten margin note:] "being black cs a sin o white ppl have more edu.

[handwritten note:] Life Changing event – mother's death

33

6

We had not seen the last of The Bitch. Auntie Beatrice appeared one day stepping up the path in the shadow of a round-bosomed, round-bottomed policewoman.

'Paper? Wha paper?' Tantie was shouting. 'I would shit on allyu paper! Yu ain't have no right! Get to Hell out mih yard!'

The stalwart policewoman spoke.

'You shut yu face!' Tantie snapped, in a brief aside, 'Whe' you come-out? I know you?' and she turned on Auntie Beatrice again.

'Allyu go an' play,' ordered Mikey.

We withdrew behind the shaddock tree, from where we could watch the proceedings like a highly animated mime perform-ance. Mikey was pulling at Tantie's arm and Tantie without her mouth stopping was jerking her shoulder and her arm to shake him off. Eventually he succeeded in drawing her aside, motion-ing to the policewoman to wait. They went inside the house and while they waited Auntie Beatrice was looking about the yard and talking to the policewoman.

Presently Mikey appeared in the gallery and looked about for us: 'Cyn-Cyn an' Toddan!' he shouted, 'come an' wash allyu foot an' put-on shoes!'

◆

The last thing they had said to us was: 'We comin for allyu just now, but don' tell them nothing, yu hear?' so we had departed with the feeling of conspirators and the brown suitcase.

Our cousins were not over-impressed with us, but neither

were we with them. When Auntie Beatrice left the room the two couples stood locked in a silent stare of scrutiny. Then Jessica darted away teasingly and placed herself behind a mound of toys in the middle of the room, informing us that we were not to touch anything, whereupon I went over and extracted a plastic teacup from the pile and walked on it. Carol screamed and Auntie Beatrice came running, exclaiming from a long way off 'Jessica! Jessica! What is happening?' and when she came in she picked Carol up and said 'What is it my baby, tell Mummy.'

I had been hoping that we'd be packed home forthwith. To my disgust Auntie Beatrice merely trapped my head in the folds of her bosom and cooed: 'You mustn't be naughty, darling.' I wrenched myself free.

That night as we lay in the strangeness I wondered when Mikey and Tantie would come for us. Mikey could come on the bike and put us on the bar . . .

'When we goin home?' Toddan's voice came peevishly.

'Jus' now,' I said with conviction. The whine in his voice had rung a bell.

'Ain't yu want Tantie?'

'Yes.'

'An Mikey?'

'Yes.'

'Well awright,' I said. 'Bawl.'

He lay still with doubt. Presently he asked: 'If I bawl we will go home?'

'Yes,' I said, quite prepared to use coercive methods, like pinching his bottom, if he wasn't going to cooperate. He was sceptical because previous experience had not shown that bawling brought any kind of desirable result – when he threw tantrums Tantie usually set him out under the furthest mango tree with instructions to cry his bellyful before he came near the house again. Thus it was that he had developed an expert bawl, for on these occasions he always made sure that we could still hear him from the house.

'Awright then,' he acquiesced at the end of his reflections.

There were no preliminaries, no revving-up. Toddan launched forthwith into a fire-siren wail that brought Auntie Beatrice running. She picked him up and kissed him on his forehead (whereupon Toddan wiped his forehead indignantly) and petted him and cooed at him, until there began to come peevish sounds from the direction of Carol's bed so she went over and petted her too. And when Auntie Beatrice produced sweets, Toddan decided to leave it at that for the time being, rejecting vigorously her offer to carry him off with Carol to sleep in her bed.

The next morning we awoke to the sound of chanting under our window. A child's voice was intoning repeatedly in the same persistent tune:

> Ca – rol
> An' Je-ssi-ca!
> Ca – rol
> An' Je-ssi-ca!

They didn't react – Carol lay with one leg cocked upon the knee of the other, contemplating her toes. And the chanting continued. Presently Toddan got up and standing on the bed leaned out of the window. The chanting stopped and Toddan stood staring for a time. Then a boy's voice: 'Ey boy, wha yu name?'

'Toddan.'

'Yu livin there now?'

'No, man, I ain' livin here. I livin by Tantie an Mikey.'

'Come an play pitch. I have a t'ousan million t'ousan million marble. An mih Ma bringing-home a t'ousan million.'

'Yu story, man,' commented Toddan.

'Well come an see nuh! I have twelve cricket-bat an forty car an an all kinda t'ing – my Ma buy them for me . . .'

At this point Auntie Beatrice swooped in and lifting Toddan down shut the window in haste.

◆

There was a violent fight every morning between Toddan and Eudora, for Toddan, whose habitual garb consisted of a vest, did not take kindly to the jersey and pants and shoes when he wasn't going anyplace.

Carol was skinny and finicky with large eyes that were perpetually languid-looking with boredom or sulkiness. At the table she calmly loaded her onion and everything else that didn't please her onto Jessica's plate. Often there was something different on her plate from what everybody else had. The first time we saw Auntie Beatrice take her spoon and feed her Toddan watched in amazement. Then he exclaimed superiorly: 'Cyntie! Yu ain' see! Cyntie! That one there' – Toddan never did bother himself with their names – 'that one there is a lil po-po!'

Bernadette was big. She set out for school on mornings importantly with a fat book-bag. She objected to Toddan's nose – she said it was too flat, and she took to calling him Flat-Nose. If she wasn't so big I'd have beaten her up.

I did beat up Carol and Jessica, every time the opportunity presented itself. Always with a view to being packed off home, it was usually Carol I attacked, pinching her or pulling one of her plaits. As a rule I waited until there was no one about, but once Jessica was there and flew at me before Auntie Beatrice could come rushing in, so that she made her entrance just at the moment when Carol was tottering backwards propelled by my right foot while the rest of me was taken up with Jessica. Once more, to my extreme annoyance, Auntie Beatrice merely parted us, shoving Jessica roughly aside, and said to me 'It's not nice to fight, dear.' Then she went to Carol, who was yowling with all her might, and kissed her and blew on the place where I'd pinched her and said never mind Mummie's baby never mind.

Jessica was bigger than Carol but she was Carol's lackey. She walked around behind her like a shadow, ran and fetched things for her, tidied up after her and helped her put her clothes on when Eudora wasn't there. Carol threw tantrums when Jessica couldn't get her shoes buckled fast enough and Auntie Beatrice came rushing in to upbraid Jessica.

Carol threw many a tantrum in the bathroom, screaming at Eudora to hurry up and get the soap off her and Eudora said 'Awright White-lady,' after which she would sometimes mutter under her breath 'You damn lil redants!' Then Carol enjoyed running all over the house naked with Eudora shouting after her: 'Come put-on yu frack! Caral! come put-on yu frack!' The day Carol started calling her dress her 'frack' Auntie Beatrice was near hysterical: 'If you can't speak properly when you speak to these children then don't bother to say anything to them at all! It's not that you never went to school in Grenada! What class did you go up to?'

'T'ird Standard, Ma'm,' replied Eudora without raising her eyes.

'Well! There you are! Third Standard! That means you could very well speak properly if you wanted to! You came over here to better yourself, girl, I don't understand why you have to go on talking like Grenadian people!'

Eudora always looked as though she were on the point of crying. She went about singing in a mournful voice the chorus

> Do' pass dey
> do' pass dey
> yu go get big-belly

and when Auntie Beatrice approached she seemd to swallow her tongue, so abruptly did the song come to an end.

But during the day when Auntie Beatrice and Uncle Norman were at work and the others at school (Auntie Beatrice said that I would go to school with Carol and Jessica soon) Eudora leaned over the bannister and talked gaily with people going up the road, laughing quite as boisterously as Tantie. Sometimes people came in to her. There was a young man who always had a matchstick in his mouth and a cap on back-to-front. He chewed the matchstick and eyed her up and down slowly with the matchstick hanging out of one corner of his mouth and the other corner stretched upwards in a saucy sneer: 'How the Seen-Giargies gal?'

'Gwan, you hear, you ever hear me say "Seen-Giargies"? I from St George's, boy, an gwan I tell you, come-out the people house, you wan' the Madam put me out on the street?'

'Let she put yu out nuh, yu could come down by me,' and he made a swipe at her as she fled giggling to the kitchen.

She carried on sullen monologues with Toddan and me as audience, to the effect that she come from a desant home in a desant parta St George's and she ain' 'custom polishing nobody floor and washin they clothes gi' them but jus wait till the Mister come and take her out of this place she swear Christmas ain' come and find her in this place for it ain' long now before the Mister come.

On many a morning we were awakened by Auntie Beatrice's suppressed scolding-voice: 'Did you come here to look for steelbandmen? Did you?'

And there was a noise like a whimper that must have been Eudora's reply.

'Well what is the meaning of that then, what is the meaning of it? This is your last chance, girl, next time it's out! Then you could go somewhere where you could mix with all the steelband-

39

men and riff-raff you want, but not while you are living in this house!'

Auntie Beatrice always called me 'Cynthia', as if I were in school. And she always called Toddan 'Codrington', and Toddan never knew she meant him. 'It was your Auntie Beatrice who gave you that name, dear,' she said to him, 'when you were a little tiny baby. Don't you think it's nicer than that silly name they call you?' Toddan usually nodded hurriedly to whatever Auntie Beatrice said to him, so as to be set free to go about his business again. But I took personal offence to her objection to Toddan's name.

'He name Toddan,' I informed her sharply. 'Is I who name him.'

'Yes, darling,' she said, with her irritating way of rolling my head into her bosom, 'but that was when you were little. You're a big girl now, aren't you?'

The little boy next door had taken to standing at the fence and chanting Toddan's name on mornings, but Toddan couldn't look out the window now because Auntie Beatrice had shifted the bed. We only played on the right hand side of the house, although the yard was wider on the other side where the little boy lived. Auntie Beatrice often came and leaned out of the window and chatted with the children over the other fence: 'How are you, dear? And how are your Mummie and Daddy?' Once the children's mother came out into the yard wearing a bathing-suit and sun-glasses and an enormous straw hat, and placed herself elaborately on a deck chair. Then Auntie Beatrice's voice came in an urgent whisper behind me: 'Cynthia dear, it's not nice to stare!' Then, clearing her throat, she called out to the woman in a tittery voice 'I see you are taking some sun?'

'Oh yes. Not used to it yet, you know – oh it's marvellous. Children have got used to it, though.'

'You will, too, just wait,' said Auntie Beatrice in the tittery voice.

'That's what my husband says to me – he thinks I'm out of my head to want to lie about in the sun. "We *shelter* from the sun," he says, "not go and *sit* in it!" But I still think it's lovely.'

The children's mother was there the afternoon when Auntie Beatrice had a gathering of a priest and ladies for whom Eudora mournfully poured out tea and went backwards and forwards with little cakes. We were all dressed up and brought forth and Auntie Beatrice said 'Here they are, Cynthia and Codrington. Say "good afternoon Father, good afternoon ladies".' We sat among them, with Toddan perched on a lady's knee. Carol eventually began to make her peevish sound and at one point to prance about the room, because all the ladies were rather taken up with Toddan. Toddan, however, was only interested in the cakes.

'What a nice watch you have, dear,' said one of the ladies.

'Mih Uncle Herman buy it for mih,' said Toddan casually, not taking his eyes off the tray.

'Your uncle what, dear?' asked Auntie Beatrice with an expression of puzzlement.

'Mih Uncle Herman, nuh.'

She looked very puzzled indeed. Then something like alarm brushed over her face.

'Oh! that's not your uncle, dear. You only have one uncle, that's your Uncle Norman.' Then she leaned forward and whispered something to the company, whose heads had converged to listen, and then the heads came apart again in a few scurrying notes of amusement that were clipped-off at the edge.

Their talking was clipped-off at the edge, too, and every now and then they fell silent, when all you could hear were the chinking of cups on saucers and Auntie Beatrice's tittery-voice proposing more sponge-cake.

Then a chinking, tittery silence was devastated by Toddan's voice.

'Ooey!' he suddenly exclaimed, springing down from the lady's lap and pulling at his clothes. 'Take off this damn stupid pants, man! Ah want to ka-ka!'

◆

One morning Auntie Beatrice suddenly came home again, marching into the house in a temper.

'Where are Cynthia and Codrington? Eudora, pack these children's things. Come children, your dear *Tantie* is taking you. God help you!'

She placed us in the gallery and as she went in again I heard a squeal from Toddan and when I turned to look he was down at the bottom of the path about to take a leap up into Mikey's arms and Tantie was right behind Mikey, all dressed up and with a hat on her head and they came up the path with Mikey carrying Toddan and kissing him again and again and Toddan reached over and firmly lifted the hat off Tantie's head, and Tantie squawked with mirth: 'A-a! the mister don' like mih wid mih hat! I bet yu see I leave yu here by yu Tantie Beatrice! An' *look* mih girl! Tee! Dou-dou!'

I was rushing down the path, distraught with joy.

All the way home Toddan talked and talked like a gramophone record. Then I spied the bakery, and he started to hop up and down, singing 'The bakery, the bakery, look the bakery there.' Then we were passing over the bridge, and then we saw the big immortelle tree at the corner and we were both hopping up and down.

That night there were macommès and compès in the house and we were sitting on Tantie's knees while she recounted the triumph.

'Well she know big-shot, yu know, big-shot in all kinda Government office, Father-priest and thing – so she get this paper. But we wipe we backside with she paper – we send the chirren to get some town-breeze, an' in that time I get a statement from Selwyn – yu shoulda see the bitch face in the Courthouse! Eh! she face look like if she panty fall-down!' There was an attack of hilarity. 'Eh! but that is the end of that bitch, matter fix, yu livin by yu Tantie, yu father self could go to Hell – wha yu say, allyu ain't even have no use for he!' and we clambered closer about her, all but strangling her, so that she squawked again.

7

We the seasoned elders at Mrs Hinds' were beginning to dis-cuss, for the benefit of the Little Ones, the proud prospect of going over to Big-school. In casual tones we considered the fact that over there you know, you sit at things called 'desks', not all around a table as if you were going to eat, and over there you read hard books, with plenty words and nearly no pictures, and you think you sing baby nursery-rhymes over there? Oh no over there you learn poetries, and you have to stand up by yourself and say them in front of the whole school, no Mary-had-a-little-lamb oh no and you think everybody sits in a little cheenky cheenky room together? Oh no there you're in a big big room, big like a house, and plenty plenty teachers and they don't let you say a word not a word not even Jumbie Jumbie dry mih slate but oh yes in Big-school you don't write on a slate no man you write on paper and don't think you can go

writing up-and-down up-and-down crapaud-foot gone-to-town
oh no . . .

The Little Ones (i.e. those who were but five, to our wizened
six) were duly impressed and we savoured our importance. But
there was not one of us who did not view with dread every one
of these proud promotions. We had none of us any desire to
quit the mild chaos of the Hinds establishment, where learning
was a vapour we breathed or did not breathe, a fortuitous by-
product of the proceedings, that like the ripples of heat in the
afternoon hovered about the heap of scraping and chanting Mr
Hinds roaring the Ol'-Lady sitting with a cloth around her head
and Mrs Hinds' endless embroidery thread; by all reports at Big-
school Learning was the main business of the day.

I arrived at Big-school on the cross-bar of Mikey's bicycle.
For the occasion he had started calling me Ma-Davis. Along the
way he pretended to run into every lamp post, dog and tree we
encountered, veering away in the nick of time and when I
screamed in alarm he stared straight ahead with his features
drawn into all gravity and said 'Whatappen, Ma-Davis?' When
we arrived at the school he hoisted me up onto his shoulders
from whence I surveyed the crowd while we waited and every
now and then he enquired: 'How the life up-there Ma-Davis?
Gord yu heavy, man, Ma-Davis. Soon I can't pick yu up at-all!'

Tantie started sending me to the shop all by myself on little
errands – a pound of sugar, a piece of pig-tail. This was an
exhilarating adventure, but it gave me a sad sinking feeling to
come into the shop in broad daylight and with hardly anyone
there. For then it looked as though the pots and comic-books
hanging down from the ceiling were fly-spotted; as though the
same two boxes of luxury chocolate had been sitting in the glass
case from as far back as I could remember, askew, waiting; and
as as though Ling were tired and absent-minded. Friday night
was shop-night. The mixed smell of chicken-feed and salt-fish,

and the smell of coarse gritty sugar so that you could almost feel the brown grains on your tongue. We sat on the piles of turgid sacks while our big-people crowded the shop, leaning on the counter as if they had come to settle down for the night, or arguing loudly with Ling or with each other; we play Red-Light or Hoop out in front on the concrete by the combined efforts of Ling's insect-besieged electric bulb and the weary street lamp, and there was never a more romantic light on earth.

Almost every Friday night there was a friendly exchange between Tantie and Ling on the subject of honesty: 'Ling, yu too thief, man, oh Gord, it never had a Chinee man thief like you!' Ling's reply was always good-natured: 'Me no thief, Miss Lrosa, all we got to live, no?' and the beam that creased his eyes and his whole face would almost conquer Tantie.

Ling still spoke what was to us a rather quaint pidgin. His wife spoke nothing at all (only Chinese) – she mostly held the fat baby, smiled amiably and helped Ling pack groceries. It was Henry, who was a miniature Ling and who was known as The Doc, who stepped into the breach when customer complaints took on a more involved nature. Even in the rum-shop he would face ominous rum-soaked companies of men, separated from them by only a flimsy plank of a counter, and coldly argue the morality of a three-cents rise on the price of a flask.

There was one time when Tantie felt herself more than bearably hard done by in the matter of groceries. The salt-fish was mostly bone, there were *three* nails in the chicken-feed, and the last straw came when, biting into a crisp warm slice of bake, she heard a horrible crunch and spat out a lily-white pebble, accompanied by a lily-white front tooth.

That Friday night when we walked into the shop customers moved aside so that Tantie could march straight up to the counter, and silence fell. This was due as much to the fact that they were familiar with the indiscriminate nature of Tantie's wrath as to the fact that a lil noise was always welcome on a Friday-night-in-the-shop, and a lil noise involving Tantie was sure to be one of the highest order.

Tantie had in her hand a paper bag containing three nails, the stone-hard remnants of a bake, a pebble and a tooth. Ling seemed to duck a few inches when he saw her coming. He started to beam in advance. Tantie grimly untwisted the paper bag and turned it upside down on the counter. The contents rolled out, the tooth lurching away from the other objects. There was a burst of laughter, quickly repressed as Tantie turned and glared at the assembled company. She turned again to the business in hand.

'What yu t'ink o' all that, Ling?' she inquired.

'How yu mean, Miss Lrosa?' asked Ling, his eyes darting nervously from the display on the counter to Tantie's face and realizing with dismay that it was not a situation to be beamed out of.

'Come Ling, do' play stupid here for me now, because you an' I know yu blasted smart! What all this was doin' in the goods? Watch that big-stone dey an' watch mih mout'!' and Tantie leaned over the counter and bared her front teeth at him, causing him to start violently; there was another burst of hilarity and while Tantie turned to glare Ling took the opportunity of hurrying out into the back of the shop in search of Henry. Henry emerged, a few paces in front of his father, bespectacled and with a pencil stuck behind his ear, looking like a preoccupied scholar annoyed at the interruption.

'Well yu could jus' send he back, I ain' come to argue wid a lil chile; go back an' do yu home-lesson, dou-dou.'

But only Tantie would conceive of calling Henry dou-dou, for you might just as well walk up and pat the Judge on the head. Ling was talking to him in Chinese, pointing at the little pile on the counter. Henry continued to look unimpressed.

'Ah say sen 'im back – yu wouldn' like me say a bad-word in front o'yu chile?'

Ling did not catch this and Henry translated rapidly for him – their eyes exchanged an amused twinkle.

'Ah, Miss Lrosa,' beamed Ling, glad of the diversion, 'my son Henry he know all bad-word already!'

'Awright, awright, wha 'bout mih teet' way fall-out?'

'Yu sure it ain' goods yu buy up the road, Miss Rosa?' Henry put the question mildly.

'Goods I buy up the road yu father head! Is now I going an buy goods up the road!'

And though we stormed out and marched up to Ramsaran, for the whole time that we traded up there Tantie always reminded me to pass in the back street, or we sneaked past Ling's door like thieves. When we went back to Ling it was the Friday night after Uncle Herman had sent Tantie to get her gold tooth put in. Tantie was in the best of humour, flashing smiles all around.

'Ah! Miss Lrosa! So yu come-back from the country! beamed Ling, with his eyes creased in joy.

'Yes, man,' said Tantie; then leaning across the counter she confided to him in a thunderous whisper: 'You pigtail sweeter!'

Ling beamed on and nodded steadily throughout the bewildering burst of hilarity.

That was the time when Mikey was in such a bad mood for days on end that Tantie used to tell him he could go and live up in the shaddock tree or in the fowl-run until he could put his face like human again and Mikey used to mutter when she was out of ear-shot you talkin 'bout human-face an yu mout' dey like the shittin' Bank o' England.

8

Big-school lived up to a great deal of our mixed expectations. Much of it was the purest exhilaration, like the feel of the crisp new copy-book with the King's head on the outside and the neat pattern of blue and red lines on the inside waiting to be overrun by the new scholarship. But there was so much we had not altogether bargained for – a teacher who was an individual who kept a sharp eye on you all the time, neither embroidering nor chatting with her mother; the menace to life and limb constituted by the presence of hordes of older children. Too much of Big-school, it seemed, was going to be sheer dismay.

We sat in a kind of well, for there were children packed onto a raised platform running around the edges of the cavernous hall that had a continuous wire-netting slit along the tops of its walls, like lavatory windows letting in dusty light in a chequered pattern over our heads. The well was filled in with a bizarre patchwork of children in thick squares that were closely wedged together but facing different directions and reciting and buzzing in contradictory tempos. Morning assembly was an uncomplicated process – we merely stood up in our places and faced one end of the hall, and when it was over we turned to our proper directions and sat down again. The whole school could never be got onto one floor, so Mr Thomas held assembly upstairs while Teacher Iris led the prayers downstairs. The problem of synchronizing the singing was given much thought and effort, but still the upstairs assembly always managed to be a line or two behind us in the hymn, so that the total effect was something in the nature of an ecclesiastical rendition of Three Blind Mice.

In the beginning the thought of all those children was alarming. There was our multitude, the lowest classes, 'down-on-the-ground' as the others said with a certain contempt. We were surrounded by the condescending benches of bigger children ranged on the platform. And over our heads, every time the bell rang, was the most terrifying thunder of feet and furniture, reminding us that upstairs were just as many children again as we could see around us, bigger and more condescending yet than the ones up on the platform.

Big-school was no place for little children. At recess-time the upstairs children materialized like doom hurtling down the back and front stairs which could barely contain the torrent. The whole building seemed to tremble. Outside we clung to the walls and hovered in sheltered places for fear of being knocked down and trampled upon by the giants galloping about their yard. The four standpipes were permanently surrounded by a knot of viciously jostling children so that there was almost no chance of us ever getting a drink of water – sometimes a bigger brother or sister would push one of us through to the tap but the younger child as often as not emerged in tears, dishevelled and drenched.

We had looked forward to playing on the Savannah as being part and parcel of Big-school. Both EC and RC children played there, and prior to our promotion how often, on our way to Mrs Hinds, we had lingered on the edges of the Savannah watching with envy the huge dancing chanting rings, the long thick skipping-ropes threshing the ground, the pounding races in which you could run until you were tired, so much space was there. Now it was clear to us that as yet to venture onto the Savannah at recess-time would be suicide.

The aspect of Santa Clara EC School, too, was decidedly less imposing than before. It had always been with a certain thrill that we had regarded this bastion of learning in its two-storeyed splendour, square and solid and firmly planted on the ground.

Now it had lost its awesomeness, for it too was plainly intimidated by all those murderous children who rode it like an old donkey, rioted and stampeded in its insides until it could burst, and battered its outsides with stones, balls, sticks, fists, rotten fruit and other hurtful objects. The walls of the school seemed to have been painted a doubtful ochre at some epoch, Government yellow, like the Police Station and the Warden's Office up in Coriaca. Those who had had cause to enter Mr Thomas' office testified, at any rate, that the walls in there were of a different colour. But the colour of Santa Clara EC School was, on the average, an intermediate shade between grey and khaki.

◆

Teacher Gloria rather alienated a section of her class at the beginning by continually referring to us as 'Missis Hindsis children.' We found this unnecessary of her. She seemed to believe that we were a bunch of infants who had wandered in from playing and who had no idea what school was all about. As if we couldn't write s the proper way round, most of us, and tell b from d.

She was a young lady with crisply ironed blouses and droopy flared skirts and who was like an over-active mother hen, directing and scolding and clucking round us all day long. But we were thoroughly annoyed at her for the way in which she would suddenly turn into a girl whenever Sir came down the stairs, and when he talked to her she either hung her head or looked up at him as though he were the Governor or we didn't know who.

On Friday afternoons she herded us cluckingly down to the Savannah where we joined Third Standard under the big-tree and she promptly flopped into a girl again as we were stirred into their midst and Sir took charge of us all. Third Standard were newly-mounted upstairs children; they ignored us with all their might.

We had games or story-reading, depending on Sir's inclination. In either case he sat in state upon a chair with his legs crossed and a tamarind whip resting delicately across his knees. We stood in the shade of the spreading tree and he read us stories about exemplary children who quailed not at the call of duty and were loth to tell a lie. Our minds floated lazily on the droning afternoon air up into the branches of the tree and across the deserted Savannah on which there still lay a little haze of unsubsided dust like its pulse still throbbing after the midday violence. At the end of the story we were sharply gathered in again for Sir suddenly pointed someone out with the whip and demanded to know what the moral of the story was.

Teacher Gloria stood at the back of the gathering with her arms piously folded. We considered her a traitress for delivering us up to Sir in this manner, letting him bark at us without the slightest remonstrance on her part. And once when we were having games he barked 'Gloria! Come here!' and both Gloria Foster and Teacher Gloria came running and Sir looked as if he would have liked to swallow his tongue but recovered and barked at Gloria Foster 'I said "*Teacher* Gloria will you kindly come here"!' and Gloria said that she had heard him say Gloria and Sir gave her a licking with the whip for rudeness and said her ears were too big and he would see and cut them down for her. And we had all heard him call Gloria, and Teacher Gloria didn't say a word.

Teacher Gloria threatened recalcitrant little boys that she would march them upstairs to be dealt with by Sir, whose readiness with the whip was proverbial. Up and down the school Third Standard was viewed as a minor Valley of the Shadow, the redoubtable initiation to upstairs, to be approached with a certain proud stoutheartedness.

9

Mr Oliver was the school watchman, and lived in a hut in one corner of the schoolyard. There was nothing in all creation that irritated and grieved Mr Oliver more than schoolchildren.

Not that he was on much better terms with the rest of creation, as many a dog or other animal who strayed into the schoolyard barely lived to tell. Mis' Dorothea fared better. She merely waddled in every day with her tray on her head and her two-legged stool under her arm, set up the tray just inside the front gate and then lowered her vast posterior with finality onto the minute stool. She hummed a contented tune to herself as she deftly rolled channa cones and filled them, peeled oranges, arranged her wares or counted her money.

Some days Mr Oliver ranted at her, but then she cocked her head on one side and sang 'Jesu lover of my soul' with grating conviction while she rolled a cone with special care, turning the piece of paper round and round between her fingers, holding it up and examining it now from one angle now from another, singing more and more earnestly as Mr Oliver's wrath increased; it was every bit like a revival meeting with the preacher fulminating and the choir in soulful competition. She ended the hymn with a full-blooded 'Arrrre-mennnn' and started from the beginning again if Mr Oliver had not yet moved off.

Sometimes he threatened to go and call the police to remove her from the school premises, and would even start down the road at an irate shuffle, looking over his shoulder every few seconds to see what effect this was producing. It never produced any effect at all, Mis' Dorothea still sat like a building, and more often than not Mr Oliver in the end slunk in through one of the side gates and went to bed.

On most days, every tactic having failed, he was reduced to shuffling to and fro before her muttering curses, like a dog prowling and stalking and fretting in a wide circle round an offensively sedate cat. When he was tired he placed himself on his box and opened up his newspaper, twitching it sharply at intervals and grunting to demonstrate that he had not softened or climbed down but that his daily newspaper was in the long run more important than an obnoxious encroaching marchan' woman. Then it was that Mis' Dorothea could be heard chatting cosily to him while she peeled her oranges and rolled her channa paper, telling him the latest on her big son George, then her half-sister down in Sierra Grande, and moving out towards the furthest twigs of her family tree. Often she did not seem to have noticed that Mr Oliver had folded up his paper and departed.

It was Mr Oliver's job to guard the school against possible burglary and generally to look after the building and grounds. He took his duties rather more seriously than was demanded of him, and had he been able would long since have emptied the school, locked all the gates and fortified the premises so that none could enter, neither man nor beast nor, above all, schoolchild. But to Mr Oliver's chagrin year after year the schoolbuilding continued to harbour schoolchildren, and their number never decreased. There was even talk of an annex being built, to accommodate even more – at least a hundred more – *schoolchildren*!

It must have been the thought and the sight of the multitudes of schoolchildren pouring through the gates morning after morning for years on end that had bent Mr Oliver's back and slowed his movements down to a slouch and given him his overall air of voluntary dilapidatedness. It was said that he had not changed his clothes for years, and slept in them. Such was their appearance at any rate. They were approximately the same colour as the schoolbuilding and like the schoolbuilding had once been of a more prepossessing colour. An untidy growth like grey stunted weeds had overrun an area of his face. One of his eyebrows was in a permanently raised position, like a disparaging question-mark as to the validity of anything whatsoever, while his eyes were never more than half open, as if he would shut out as much as was possible of the disgusting spectacle which the world presented. His mouth was stretched into a sneer which was as often as not frothy at the corners. Older children said that Mr Oliver had been known to smile, when his daughter and grandchild visited him, but we seriously doubted the existence of these personages.

Our primary grievance concerning Mr Oliver was the fact that his hut had been built right under the pommerac tree. Mr Oliver in theory slept for a part of the day, but it was a sleep which permitted him not only to hear the squelch of a pommerac falling onto his roof, but to distinguish between the squelch of a pommerac fallen due to natural causes and the squelch of a pommerac whose fall had been provoked by the hand of a schoolchild. In the latter case one heard an angry roar from the interior of the hut and came away as rapidly as possible.

But Mr Oliver very rarely succeeded in catching hold of a schoolchild, far less in carrying out any of his grisly promises on us. He shuffled discontently backwards and forwards through the yard carrying a shovel or a broom on his shoulder and murmuring at us through his teeth: 'Shit-hounds, damn lil shit-hounds.' Often the broom was brandished, and sometimes thrown, but years of practice had not improved his aim, and it was with great enjoyment that we watched from a safe distance the wheezing creaking process of Mr Oliver bending over to pick up his broom and then straightening up again. And then it became a game.

The game was begun by Carlyle Joseph and a group of his admirers. Carlyle Joseph it was of whom folk said that only the Grace of God and a daily licking could ever retrieve him from the Devil, and on whose bottom Sir had once broken three tamarind whips in succession, each time sending him out to pick a new one.

Carlyle Joseph and the others would follow Mr Oliver at a few yards' distance dancing and singing and beating on tin cans. When Mr Oliver halted in his tracks and turned around to curse them they scurried in all directions, laughing. When he had turned and started on his way again they crept up behind him once more and continued. Before long all the children round about left what they were playing at and came flocking like beasts of prey to the sound of Mr Oliver's raving. Soon there was a wide chanting circle about him and sooner or later he began to throw his broom, at which we scattered shrieking with relish, watched him retrieve it and then closed in again for more. It was only the sudden appearance of a teacher which could bring the game to a stop.

One day the game was in full swing, Mr Oliver had thrown the broom at least six times, the crowd was thickening and its roar racked the walls of the empty schoolbuilding; as yet no teacher had got wind of the game; Carlyle Joseph was thrilling us to bits by performing one daring act after another – dancing upon the fallen broom until Mr Oliver had shuffled crazedly to within inches of it, creeping right up behind him and poking a stick at his bottom, and at each prank we screamed with trepidation. We were closing in again, chanting 'Run run run, look the jumbie-man', and Mr Oliver was hoarse now and there was froth at the corners of his mouth and he was turning round and round and jabbing at the air with the broom as he shouted incoherently when suddenly his mouth stood open and the broom clattered to the ground at his feet. A thick, glistening streak was starting down Mr Oliver's forehead. Shock travelled swiftly from those who saw to the rest of the mob and there was an abrupt silence as the breath went out of us. We stood and stared for a few seconds. And then just as abruptly we began to scream and run in opposite directions, in circles, to and from the scene of the crime, round and round the schoolbuilding.

Mr Oliver was shuffling about again within a few days, his head still swathed in bandages. We were informed for our edification that Mr Oliver had been offered a transfer but that his loyalty to Santa Clara EC was such that he would not hear of it.

There was no doubt as to Carlyle Joseph having thrown the stone. He was expelled, belaboured by his father and then by his big brother, whereafter they put him in the Orphanage.

10

RC School and EC School had morning, midday and afternoon recess at the same hours. As the clanking of the two bells climbed strugglingly into the air the Savannah held its breath. The clanking petered out again and there was a treacherous lull; then a stridency was approaching like wind-driven rain. In another moment the two far fringes of the Savannah had come alive and were running, running headlong to meet each other – on one side the turbulence spilling across the grass teemed with maroon, white and khaki, on the other with brown, cream and khaki; the space between was being steadily sucked up. Then one side gained the middle with jubilant shouting and dancing whereupon the other halted, withdrew a certain distance and both halves of the Savannah fell to their normal activity. But frequently the two front lines arrived at the middle simultaneously, which is to say collided, when there was a fierce and prolonged riot, often lasting until once more the clanking struggled out over the Savannah, when the colours extricated themselves from each other and drained away reluctantly in opposite directions.

The middle part of the Savannah was No-man's-land, it belonged to whichever side got there first. There was nothing special about this part, there were choicer spots, like under the big-tree or down in the gully. There was really no reason, either, why EC or RC children should not play on whichever side of the Savannah they pleased. The Savannah was public property and no authority had ordained its division into separate playgrounds. But EC and RC children were sworn to eternal enmity, and firmly resolved to keeping apart on the Savannah.

To us it was simply in the nature of things that we should be at war with RC School. And then it was so exciting, we would not have wished it otherwise. When one came to think of it RC children were not all that unbearably barbarous and unthinkable. Many of them were neighbours and cousins and sisters and brothers. I sometimes tried to imagine what took place in a house where both EC and RC children lived. Did they not speak to each other when they came home on afternoons until they had changed their clothes? And on mornings were they friends while they brushed their teeth and washed, but stopped talking abruptly the minute they had got into their respective uniforms?

The colour of our girls' uniform was a sore point for the RC children struck an unfortunate comparison and delighted in calling us the 'ka-ka sisters' or 'too-too-cake'. There was no direct answer to this, but then we could retrieve a measure of dignity by reminding them that our school was newer than theirs and theirs was only made of wood, which made theirs a shanty-town school.

But the wretched RC children seemed to have altogether too much with which they could crow over us and give themselves airs. Almost every year they managed to win one more exhibition to secondary school than we did, and as sure as rain when we won none at all it was a bumper year for them – four, five, six RC faces grinning like jackasses out of *The Herald*. And too often they won just a few more prizes at Inter-School sports and a point or a half-point more at the singing competitions (of course it was all on account of their nuns and Fathers working obeah with Mary-statues and candles in the Catholic Church, as everybody knew).

So all was at stake on the middle part of the Savannah, three times a day. There were other forms of warfare. Once in a while someone was waylaid by children from the other school, but this could end in lickings and expulsions. Every now and then, as for example when a cricket-ball landed on the other side and was confiscated, the two halves of the Savannah would rear up and stand on end for an eternity facing each other over the precarious strip in the middle, and the air was alive with danger. There was even known to have been a gigantic free-for-all, once upon a time, when frantic teachers and nuns and priests turned out in full force and spent a desperate hour darting about capturing children and stuffing them into their respective schools until they had succeeded in clearing the Savannah.

But the most thrilling tactic was what we called the Dip-Over-an'-Double-Back. A strong-armed group from one side would dart into enemy territory, whisk in among them, wind and thread audaciously through the games on their frontier, and be pounding home again before the others were able to react. They were given a boisterous reception, with exultant clapping and cheers and booing across at the duped enemy.

But these missions did not always end thus satisfyingly. Sometimes men were caught. There would be a huge heaving pile on the ground with shrieking and swearing and arms and legs, while the other side watched in horror. Sooner or later above the huddle, like a flag on a mountaintop, was hoisted a sorry pair of khaki trousers. The huddle disintegrated like a cake into dancing crumbs; the khaki flag was seen jabbing at the sky on the end of a stick, darting swiftly about followed closely by a bare-bottomed boy who might have been in the final stages of insanity and who in turn was followed by a joyful throng.

11

We ascended into Third Standard. Sir received us on high with a lengthy booming harangue, clearing his throat and pacing grandly to and fro with his hands joined behind his back or tapping the whip against his leg, rocking on his heels, now and then half-sitting on a corner of the table as he twirled his mustache, pausing for long seconds at a time with his head cocked on one side as if to savour the echo of what he had said before. We were further over-whelmed, as well as vaguely flattered, by the incomprehensibility of his utterances.

This performance proved to be a regular feature. Sir was given to discoursing on things called 'Seemliness' and 'Constancy' and 'Veracity' and others. We had to sit as immobile as furniture, for a falling pencil, a sneeze or a fidgeting child made him forget what it was he was going to say, and by the time he had finished roaring with anger he had also forgotten where it was he had broken off, so that he was obliged to begin several paragraphs back, or sometimes from the very beginning.

Across the top of the blackboard was a permanent inscription in multicoloured chalk: THE DISCIPLE IS NOT GREATER THAN THE MASTER. It was written in flowery letters which Sir spent ages repairing when they became the slightest bit faded, stepping back and holding his head on one side to admire each curl he performed. Offenders were sentenced to writing out this row of words a hundred times, an exercise which did not add to anyone's enlightenment as to their significance.

The inscription was also our model text when we had Penmanship. Painfully we copied letter by letter – necks strained upward to their absolute limit of elasticity and eyes narrowed, then a nervous pencil gripped with such intensity that often the letter appeared on the following page, and finger-joints were sore for a long time afterwards. Sir moved about among us with his hands clasped behind his back, wagging the whip. Often the whip descended with terrible suddenness upon a back hunched tensely over its copy-book; Sir did not brook 'upstartedness' in the young, nor letters that did not bear a suitable likeness to the model script.

Sir called his whip 'Fire and brimstone' or 'The wrath of God'. He and the whip were inseparable – he used it to point things out on the blackboard; he waved it in the air or tapped on the table with it during his speeches; it lay across the table in front of him as he sat and read to us tales of unvanquished knights with valiant swords and trusty steeds; with it he liberally dispensed both the wrath of God and fire and brimstone. But there were times when he relinquished it.

From time to time there blew a silence across the whole floor. Sometimes it started out of a commotion of one kind or another in a class. Often it was purely accidental and unaccountable, 'an angel passing'. But sometimes it spread from one of the two doors at either end of the floor, where Mr Thomas had suddenly appeared, or the Reverend had come to smile on us and pat random heads. Then it was that Sir edged backwards and eased the whip onto his chair or slid it under papers on his table, or on a few desperate occasions it slithered to the floor.

And when either of them appeared in the middle of a roaring, then a curious process took place before us. Sir's eyes shooting crimson out of his head seemed to scurry in behind eyelids lowered a little like shutters, his forehead flattened itself, the bristling mustache lay down, and the roaring tailed off as his mouth was seen to roll swiftly out across his face like a mat.

Sir drilled us regularly and violently in the Art of Noiselessly Rising from our seats: one afternoon a week we spent getting up and sitting down, getting up and sitting down without interruption (sometimes the recess bell rang and the rest of the floor drained away from around our class still bobbing up and down) while Sir stamped about and roared and banged the whip on the table and on our desks and on us until we could 'gently rise up as with one will' (the little choir-boys of Westminster Abbey of six, seven and eight years were trained to do this, he had read or imagined, so there was no possible alternative open to us) instead of making a 'din and sore confusion that calls to mind Coriaca Market on a Sunday morning'.

We looked forward to Mr Thomas visiting our class. For as he approached not only did Sir relinquish the whip, but fiercely beaming at us he motioned to us to stand up, whereupon without fail Mr Thomas impatiently waved us down again, but already we had started up in the most joyful pandemonium of scraping, banging benches, rulers and books and pencils clattering to the floor, shuffling feet (those with shoes coming into full play), before we slowly crashed to our seats again in a relayed thunder.

And all the while Sir smiling for all he was worth – the smile only became wavy around the edges as Mr Thomas began to move away, and not until he was through the door and out of sight for some time did Sir begin to roar. Mr Thomas had so much to think about that he sometimes forgot things and had to come up the steps again to say something he had remembered on the way down.

12

I had only ever raided the Estate in Mikey's company, for there was danger about, blood-curdling danger. For Mr Brathwaite who lived in the depths of the acres and acres of Santa Clara Estate was a spirit. Centuries and centuries ago he had killed a woman, a very beautiful woman who was a servant in the Estate house, and the woman's man had worked an obeah on him so he couldn't die. At full moon he turned into a lagahou and by the light of the moon met the woman, who had naturally meanwhile turned into a djablesse.

Some said he had gone mad and killed and eaten his wife and all his children, too, so that having got the taste of children he was simply dying for a fat Santa Clara child to eat, which he would get if we couldn't behave.

On many an evening after we had played we would huddle together on a doorstep and envelop ourselves with a kind of fascinated horror as we retold and elaborated upon the super-natural wickedness of Mr Brathwaite. None of us had ever seen him, so there was none to contradict the descriptions of his long pointed teeth and green eyes that shot bullets; one of us would recall how Mr Brathwaite sometimes turned into a man and walked about offering children sweets and when they came near him he grabbed them and popped them into a bag and they could be heard screaming as he dragged them through the streets away into the bowels of the old mansion.

On such an evening there were many who were terrified of extricating themselves from the hypnotized cluster and making their way home. So we went in a bunch, accompanying the littlest to their doorsteps, the biggest or bravest staying till last, when each would make a breathless dash for his house.

Now I had taken to raiding the Estate in bands of my contemporaries. We stoned the trees or poked the fruit down with rods and some foolhardy ones climbed trees. Specially appointed look-outs kept watch, thrilling with fear and too often stampeding us into mad squealing flight leaving behind a precious trail of tamarind or cerises, only to discover that Mr Brathwaite was nowhere to be seen.

The day Mr Brathwaite came upon us it was the silence that caught my attention – I was so busy collecting tamarind that I didn't know when the others had vanished. I looked up and there was a man approaching through the trees; he was a few yards away and I was facing him, paralysed. Then I heard my voice: 'Marche-shoo!' I was hissing wildly. 'Marche-shoo whitey-cockroach! Whitey-kinkalay!' but he was still coming.

So then I summoned to my rescue every obscenity I could think of, and let fly like a machine-gun. He stood stock still and his mouth fell open. Then I ran. And run I could, for even Tantie couldn't catch me in critical moments.

◆

The next morning at school there was the greatest agitation just before prayers. For standing on the platform beside Mr Thomas was Mr Brathwaite. Those who knew who he was whispered the word around so that the whole school was soon agog with expectation. Not so myself and the others who had been on the raid the day before. Mr Thomas was looking irritated.

'This is Mr Brathwaite, children,' he said, 'and there is one of you who knows why he is here. Mr Brathwaite would like to point out the child.'

We all held our breaths while Mr Brathwaite scanned the savannah of faces. There was nobody tall in front of me so there was little I could do.

'There!' he said triumphantly. 'That one with the red bows.' I scowled up at him.

'Thank you, Mr Brathwaite,' said Mr Thomas, 'we will look into the matter,' and he bade me visit his office after prayers.

◆

I was sitting in the office when Mr Thomas came in, and he placed himself at his desk without seeming to notice me. Then he looked around the room and caught sight of me.

'What is your name, child?'

'Cynthia Davis.'

'Ah! yes!' he gave a kind of chuckle. 'How is your Tantie, child?'

'Well, thank you, Mr Thomas.'

'I was your Tantie's teacher, you know, do you know that?'

'Yes.'

He chuckled the same chuckle. He was shovelling through papers, peering closely at some only to push them away hurriedly and shovel some more.

'You know your Tantie used to cuss-down Tom Dick and

Harry, too, as a schoolgirl. She would have given the Governor a cussing if he'd looked at her too hard!' he chuckled contentedly. 'Even the Headmaster was a little afraid of her.'

This reminiscence tailed off into a murmur and Mr Thomas forgot about me.

'Well, what must I do with you, child?' he said to me after a time, over the top of his glasses. 'Tell you to leave the mister's fruit trees in peace. I use' to stone those very trees, yu know, when I was a boy.' He chuckled into his mess of papers. 'Collect' some good cut-tail, too.'

He forgot me again. After a long spell of rustling he seemed to discover me once more with some surprise.

'A-a. Go to your class, child, go to your class.'

The class would be awaiting my entrance. And the other culprits would be wetting their pants expecting to be summoned to the office at any moment. I floated into the class with triumph on my face, meant for the forty-odd pairs of vulture-eyes. I didn't even give Sir a thought. And I should have. Triumph was the one thing Sir didn't stand for on a child's face. His voice barked out to trip me up.

'You there!' We stood regarding each other for a long moment while I endeavoured to adjust my features into contriteness. 'Well! what have you got to say for yourself?'

I considered the affair was closed and none of his damn business, so I exchanged the contrite look for blankness. He was in favour of blankness on your face – a good inane cow-expression.

'Well, tell us about your escapade up on other people's property!'

I was sure the hateful creature had also raided the Estate when he was little. But the picture of Sir a little boy running around in short pants wasn't feasible. He had been born complete with his mustache and the bald area on his head like the middle part of the Savannah where skipping-ropes and cricket kept the grass away. I stared at him without saying a word, until he barked: 'Come here! Put out your hand! If your parents don't teach you respect then I will!'

Every one knew that Sir gave you two lashes with the tamarind whip and then paused to see the effect. If you looked sufficiently distressed he followed up with two more and then you could go. But if you did not react satisfactorily then he went on, stopping after every two blows to scrutinize your face.

Each time he paused and looked at me he only encountered my eyes staring back at him with an intense coolness. He was furious. He began to punctuate his blows with out-of-breath snatches of barking.

'Disrespect! . . . Disrespect! . . . Up into the gentleman's land . . . to revile him! Disrespect! . . . Keep your rudeness for your mother and father!'

As he hit and hit frantically it occurred to me that perhaps Sir too thought that Mr Brathwaite was a transcendent spirit and was afraid that some terrible blight was going to fall upon us all because I had somehow offended all the gods together.

At length I decided to bawl. I let out a tearless, toneless and prolonged ship's horn blast – Sir was thrown off-balance, for all activity stopped in the other classes and everyone fumed to look at us. And I bellowed on, wickedly, suddenly hitting upon the idea of introducing elements of tune into it. There was relieved, muffled giggling from the class. Sir looked behind him nervously again and again as though he expected Mr Thomas to appear at any minute and collar him. With his eyes still darting about he dispatched me hurriedly to my seat and barked at the class to open their reading books page twenty.

I was keenly satisfied, although I was aware that I would probably not be able to use my hand for the rest of the day.

13

It must have been about in Third Standard that Helen came into existence. For by then I used to look forward to the library van on Saturdays with the greatest of impatience, having usually read the two books by Monday morning.

Books transported you always into the familiar solidity of chimneys and apple trees, the enviable normality of real Girls and Boys who went a-sleighing and built snowmen, ate potatoes, not rice, went about in socks and shoes from morning until night and called things by their proper names, never saying 'washicong' for plimsoll or 'crapaud' when they meant a frog. Books transported you always into Reality and Rightness, which were to be found Abroad.

Thus it was that I fashioned Helen, my double. She was my age and height. She spent the summer holidays at the sea-side with her aunt and uncle who had a delightful orchard with apple trees and pear trees in which sang chaffinches and blue tits, and where one could wander on terms of the closest familiarity with cowslips and honeysuckle. Helen loved to visit her Granny for then they sat by the fireside and had tea with delicious scones and home-made strawberry jam... Helen entered and ousted all the other characters in the unending serial that I had been spinning for Toddan and Doolarie from time immemorial.

At one time I took to putting on shoes the moment I woke up on mornings and not removing them again until bedtime. This caused some hilarity in the household – 'What happen, Ma-Davis, yu really takin'-in with ol'-age, eh?'enquired Mikey solicitously. But when one day I started to put on socks to go to the shop, Tantie was not amused.

'Look, Madam, when yu start to wash yu own clothes then yu could start to play the monkey – you ever put-on socks to go down in the shop? What it is take yu at-all?'

I loved rainy mornings, for then I could pretend it was winter as I left for school bundled up in an old jacket.

Helen wasn't even my double. No, she couldn't be called my double. She was the Proper Me. And me, I was her shadow hovering about in incompleteness.

For doubleness, or this particular kind of doubleness, was a thing to be taken for granted. Why, the whole of life was like a piece of cloth, with a rightside and a wrongside. Just as there was a way you spoke and a way you wrote, so there was the daily existence which you led, which of course amounted only to marking time and makeshift, for there was the Proper daily round, not necessarily more agreeable, simply the valid one, the course of which encompassed things like warming yourself before a fire and having tea at four o'clock; there were the human types who were your neighbours and guardians and playmates – but you were all marginal together, for there were the beings whose validity loomed at you out of every book, every picture (often there were Natives and Red Indians and things, but these were for chuckles and for beating back, to bring you once more the satisfaction that Right prevaileth always just before THE END), the beings whose exemplary aspect it was that shone forth to recommend at you every commodity proposed to your daily preference, from macaroni to the Kingdom of Heaven.

Helen was outgrown and discarded somewhere, in the way that a baby ceases to be taken up with his fingers and toes.

14

Mikey had a job on the Base. He used to come home laden with glossy magazines and comic-books, sometimes with great slabs of meat he said they were going to throw away. And whenever it was a bottle of anything he would drop the bike halfway up the path in his haste to get inside and tease Tantie with it, making her guess what it was before he drew it forth from a paper bag.

'What yu think the boy bring-home today?' he panted, his eyes bright with jubilation.

'I ain' know,' said Tantie. 'He mus'-be bring-home two dead-crapaud he find up the road.'

'Bet yu see I go an throw it in the river an bring two dead-crapaud!'

'Yu want to see yu Nennen jump in the river an drown she-self?'

And when he produced the bottle Tantie's squawk of delight would put him in a good mood for a week.

Then one night he came home and announced that his boss was so impressed with him that he was getting him to New York. Tantie started as if she had been hit. Then she collected herself and continued wiping the table.

'They don' much like black-people up-there, yu know,' she said casually.

'Wha yu talking, Nen, I ain' goin in the Sout'!'

'I tell yu they don' like black-people, Nort' or Sout', do' make no difference!'

'God man, Nen, is a whiteman sendin' mih! Yu think all the

white-people an them does go 'bout wid gun lookin' for black-
man to shootdown?'

'Awright, go, haul yu arse,' said Tantie heatedly. 'Yu go have
all the pretty-shirt an saga-pants yu want, go!'

'But I ain' goin for good, Nennen, I comin'-back!'

Tantie stopped wiping and glared at him.

'Yes, yu comin-back, yu comin-back when I ol' and blind, yu
comin-back for a week to sun yu backside and run-back, an yu
parkin, yuself in Strandview Hotel for the time!'

She stalked into the kitchen and we heard a violent clattering
of pots. Mikey sank into a chair and sat looking despondently
at some papers which he had in his hand. Silence reigned, except
for Tantie's angry pots.

We ate in silence. Tantie did not turn on the radio for 'Mary
Price, Midlands housewife, mother and confidante' which she
always said was damn shit but which she listened to every
evening of the week, cheupsing her contempt throughout. Mikey
did not eat very much, nor did he disappear into the night
immediately after we had eaten. Tantie cleared the table fiercely
and then there was a further spell of clanging and crashing
coming from the kitchen; at the end of which she emerged
brusquely and attacked various unnecessary tasks with
unnecessary vigour, at the same time launching into a sustained
monologue.

'But what the arse it is you have to do up-there, what the shit
up-there have to do wid you?'

She was battering imaginary dust off chairs, rubbing at a
brass plant-pot as if she wanted to annihilate it.

'Wha you put up-there, yu put some-ting up-there? Me ain'
know what you understan it have up-there – it ain' have no
blasted Heaven here but it ain' have that no-whe'-is allabout
have ketch-arse – any damn place yu is you does have to haul
yu arse out the bed when the mornin' come; yu vest does ha' to

wash yu ears does get wax an' if yu ain' shit yu belly does hurt yu. Me ain' know if you think yu does come different like if yu cross-over the blasted Jordan or what. Look that arse Selwyn – gone to sea, he gone to sail – firs' day the ship touch England, he 'basourdi, nothing to get he back on that ship – he think he reach the Golden Gates. Park he arse there, an' what, ketchin he tail, ketchin his royal arse – he ain' say so; nobody does send down from the Golden Gates to say they ketchin dey tail, for they would sound like the livin jackass. An one day outa the clear blue sky he go write an say send the chirren. Sen the chirren up in the Golden Gates wid me. Sen them to ketch they backside up in the Golden Gates wid me. Well he damn lie – he go have to come wid God and He Mother.'

And with a final vehement whack of the duster on an unoffending chair, Tantie marched into the kitchen again.

After a long time she emerged again heading for the bedroom.

'Nennen . . .' Mikey seemed to cringe as she swung round.

'Nennen I have a paper . . .' he dried up again.

'An' what?' snapped Tantie.

'They gimme this paper an well they say that them that responsible for me have to sign it . . .'

Tantie fumed and continued on her way with a loud cheups.

'I ain' know what yu tellin me that for, I ain' responsible for you, you is a big long young-man!'

To our extreme horror and consternation tears sprang into Mikey's eyes; he called after Tantie in a voice that was choked with desperateness and rage: 'But it because I ain't have twenty-one years yet! That is why!'

Tantie stopped, made her way back to where Mikey sat, and spoke to him in a trembling voice.

'Yu ain't have twenty-one years yet. Is yesterday I put yu on mih back an bring yu here. An we come till we live like two man-rat in the same hole; but that ain' say yu have to pick-up an go from me now before I even see yu grow. But hand me them paper, I can't stop yu.'

◆

Toddan was chattering too much, asking silly questions; finally he went off to explore the fountain and the tourist-shop. Uncle Sylvester was making knowing comments on propellers and immigration officers' caps.

We had never seen Mikey in a suit before, so that from the moment he had emerged from his room looking like a stark photograph he had ceased to belong to us. Now he was fumbling with baggage and papers, his hands trembling, and failing miserably to cope with the multiplicity of bags (containing an assortment of what Tantie considered to be absolute necessities for this voyage into the desert, from tamarind-jam and pone to coconut oil) and large envelopes some of which slipped and fell from him, to be scrambled up again with jerky, over-hurried movements. At one point I thought he was going to drop everything on the shiny floor and cry.

15

Tantie was still going about looking dazed and absent-minded – occasionally calling Toddan 'Mikey' and forgetting what my name was – when the first of Mikey's parcels arrived. There were a dress and stockings and a handbag for her, and toys and sweets for us. When everything had been unpacked, lying at the bottom of the box was a large photograph of Mikey; Tantie drew it out slowly as if she were afraid it would disintegrate before her eyes. She held it at arm's length and stood staring at it for a long time.

'Look mih boy,' she said to herself, 'Michael.'

Mikey sent parcels at regular intervals and Tantie used to say but a-a like all the boy gone there for is to send t'ing give he Nennen.

We were in Exhibition Class; then I sympathized with the chickens Tantie put in the cage to fatten up for Christmas.

One night I woke up because Tantie was shaking me. The light was on and she was looking most alarmed. She said I'd been reciting 'textiles, mutton, wheat . . .'

And Mr Thomas was most understanding when in a geographical treatise I revealed that the West Riding of Yorkshire was a huge race-course, in fact the largest in the world. He said he would have to put that one in his Exhibition-Class book. (Sir, on the other hand, used to suffer painful seizures, almost prancing up and down with offended horror when similar lacunae revealed themselves in our awareness of the self-evident, the fundamental and the essential. Once in a dictation nearly the whole class had either spelt 'sleet' wrong or left an inglorious blank, and he had lined us up and given us each three with the tamarind-whip for not knowing how to spell it, and six more because none could offer any suggestion as to what 'sleet' might be.)

We were coming to school at seven o'clock in the morning and the afternoon ended at six o'clock. Mr Thomas often sent us out to play in the middle of lessons, but indiscreet mention by anyone of the word 'exam' was enough to plough a weight of lead into any game.

Mr Thomas told us to leave all our books at home the day before the exam, and he would read us some good ones out of his Exhibition-Class book. It was a light headed day, and the exam was so near now as to be almost harmless. But perhaps we still laughed too loudly at Mr Thomas' prize collection of scholarly howlers; we screamed with laughter even when we didn't see the joke. We talked about what clothes we were wearing to the exam. We sang songs, 'Men of Harlech', 'The Minstrel Boy', 'Loch Lomond' – again too boisterously.

Then we talked about high-school, about which one we were going to go to, and a rowdy argument ensued, the boys contending among themselves as to whether Ascension or Imperial College was the superior institution, while the girls screamed their defence of either Queen Victoria's or St Ann's; as if we were not aware, all forty-three of us, that about forty-one of us, if not forty-three, were going to sit up in Coriaca Government School the next day and write on paper for hours to no possible end.

◆

One Sunday morning the dogs were barking frantically and someone was rattling the gallery gate. Above the din a voice said: 'But wha the arse? The people an them ain' even wake-up self! Rosa yu lazy bitch yu mean yu ain't even wake-up an buy papers yet?'

Tantie got up in haste and went and poked her head out of the window.

'A-a, Mavis, is you? But look my cross. Big Sunday-mornin, sun ain' good wipe-out the yampee out he eye yet, an you come to break-down people house!'

'Whe' Cyntie, man, the chile name in the papers an allyu dey sleepin like dead-people.'

'What yu talkin?' breathed Tantie. 'Scholarship?'

'Wha'yu t'ink, robbery wid violence?'

Tantie's squawk must have been heard up in Pointe d'Espoir.

◆

People started arriving within a few hours, and we killed chickens and Moonie came over to to help with the cooking. By evening Tantie was so merry that when there was a polite knock and Auntie Beatrice's voice said 'Can I come in and congratulate the scholar?' Tantie said heartily 'Come in, come in, whe' yu man, bring he too! Everybody have to drink on mih chile!' Toddan was sent down to the car to call Uncle Norman while Auntie Beatrice cornered me.

When she'd exclaimed at how much I'd grown, and had congratulated and kissed me, she asked me, as if between conspirators: 'And what school would you like to go to, dear, the very best, of course, for a bright girl like you – St Ann's, not so?'

'Yes.'

'Ah. Well we must talk to your Auntie. Your Uncle Norman and I can get you into St Ann's.'

A little later on, when the merriment was at its height, I saw her talking to Tantie, and Tantie was nodding and waving her hand. At a particular stage of rum Tantie tended to nod and wave her hand at whatever was said to her.

Auntie Beatrice and Uncle Norman left shortly afterwards, and Auntie Beatrice said 'See you soon, dear,' and kissed me a conspiratorial kiss.

◆

That week Tantie went around looking dazed. She was as silent and subdued as she had been loud and merry on Sunday.

Auntie Beatrice came back one day to finalize arrangements.

'Of course she will come home at vacations, and now and then at weekends,' said Auntie Beatrice.

Tantie nodded. She sat with her lips pursed and there was only one moment when I thought that her politeness would depart: Auntie Beatrice said that they would get my uniforms, of course.

'Well thank you Madam, but we will see about that,' replied Tantie sharply, 'we are not paupers.'

They came to collect me the night before school opened. Auntie Beatrice had expressed her willingness to come for me a week in advance, so I could settle down you know and get used to – but Tantie had cut her short. And before we left Tantie again reminded her that I was to come home for Moonie's wedding.

Tantie stood in the gallery with her arms folded while Toddan and Doolarie came down to the bottom of the path to peer into the car.

16

Sitting in state upon the bed Carol referred to me only as 'she'.

'I don't know where *she* is going to put her things because all my dorncing-things are in there and I have nowhere else to put them.'

'But I said you were to clear a place for her, take out those dancing-things and bring them to me, I'll find a place for them.'

Carol sat.

'Come on now, darling, Cynthia is going to be your new sister, you know that.'

'Pooh,' said Carol as she uncurled her legs and stepped down from the bed with a loud stamp, to flounce over to the wardrobe. She extracted a tangled mass of frilliness and snarled strings and flung them sulkily onto the floor. Jessica looked on with a strange kind of disgust.

Auntie Beatrice went off with the bundle and I began to unpack. Soon I discovered that there was muffled giggling at each garment I drew out of the suitcase. I was completely disconcerted. I hastily shut the suitcase although it was still half full, and stood pretending to be arranging my things in the wardrobe. They continued to sit and look on. I wondered how in the world I had ever thought to approach these two young ladies, far less beat them up, a few years before.

Then there was some whispering and then Carol's voice came forth out of a giggling: 'Uhm ... what's your name again? I can't remember – Agatha or Emmalina?' and they giggled together again. Tears blinded me.

'Oh dear, she has no tongue,' said Carol when there was no answer. 'I really must go and have a chat with Sus'n, it's boring up here,' and with that she departed, followed by Jessica.

Then there was a mild commotion at the bottom of the stairs in which I heard Auntie Beatrice's voice, then footsteps running up the stairs, and Auntie Beatrice appeared panting.

'It was very naughty of them to leave you by yourself, come and sit in the living-room until dinner is ready, dear.'

I indicated dumbly that I hadn't finished unpacking.

◆

At dinner I had no appetite and Auntie Beatrice piled things onto my plate. Carol chattered about what she and her friend

Sus'n had talked about on the phone, waving her fork in the air and dancing about on her chair. Her voice was far away and unreal, like everything else; I seemed to be looking into somebody's window. Bernadette made a brief appearance enveloped in a frothy yellow bathrobe and face-cream, and sitting sideways speared up two mouthfuls of food before she floated away again.

'Bernadette,' Auntie Beatrice called plaintively after her, 'couldn't we eat like a family, sometimes?'

'Uh-uh,' mumbled Bernadette from half-way up the stairs, 'busy'.

After some minutes the telephone rang. Carol dropped her fork with a clang and pushed her chair back so that it made a loud granting noise and precipitated herself towards the ringing, but at the same moment the yellow froth tumbled down the stairs again, with a toothbrush in her mouth, and two hands stretched out for the receiver. Bernadette pressed down on it while Carol tried to lift it, and the ringing mingled deafeningly with loud muffled sounds from Bernadette and Carol's shrieking protest. Auntie Beatrice put her hands to her ears and screamed 'Norman! Do something!' then she fanned herself distraughtly and laid her hand on her heart, murmuring 'they will kill me, they will kill me!'

Uncle Norman cheupsed and rose slowly. Meanwhile Bernadette had picked up the phone and was making unintelligible sounds into it and holding Carol off with one arm, while twisting her neck in all directions to keep Carol from getting hold of the receiver, Carol never ceasing to shriek and claw at her.

The call was for Uncle Norman. Auntie Beatrice continued to fan herself and shake her head. She shut her eyes briefly, as if in pain. Carol went and curled up in an armchair and opened a magazine.

'Don't you want any more dinner, Carol?' asked Auntie Beatrice in a weak voice. There was no answer. Bernadette came past the table on her way back to the stairs and stopped behind Auntie Beatrice's chair. Holding her bathrobe together with one hand she took the toothbrush out of her mouth and leaned over to hiss at Auntie Beatrice: 'I find it's time you started training that little bitch!' Then she floated up the stairs. Auntie Beatrice had started violently and turning around heavily in her chair she pleaded up the stairs: 'How can you talk to me like that, Bernadette?!'

Bernadette, before disappearing from view, leaned over the bannister and hissed again through her toothpaste: 'Teach that woman some manners or I will find somewhere else to live!'

This seemed to further devastate Auntie Beatrice. Carol sent a mocking singsong noise up to Bernadette.

Uncle Norman was coming back from the phone.

'You don't hear how these children talk to me, Norman, you don't hear anything at all in this house! Uncle Norman eyed her curiously and sat down to finish his food.

All this had served to take me out of myself; I had been looking on in astonishment and bewilderment. But when Auntie Beatrice put her arms around me and began to coax me to eat again, the tears I had been fighting with earlier came back again and threatened to descend. She kept her arm around me as if to protect me from the madness all around. And, I thought, to protect herself from the madness all around.

Although I resented her knowing that I was on the point of tears, I was grateful that she took me upstairs to the bedroom ahead of the others. I was sleeping in the same room as Jessica, and Carol and Bernadette shared a room. On that first night it was comforting that Auntie Beatrice firmly patrolled the two rooms while we got ready for bed. And when we were in bed and she kissed me on my forehead I could not wait until she was out of the room before I rolled over and buried my face in the pillow.

It was the first time in my life, too, that I was to sleep in a bed all by myself.

◆

The next morning I got into my blue and white uniform that Tantie had remarked with a cheups was 'damn nun-clothes'. Auntie Beatrice said how nice I looked. Carol and Jessica 'took' me to school, all the way walking miles away from me and from each other. They abandoned me entirely before we entered the gate.

The courtyard was a buzzing, shifting blue-and-whiteness. Young ladies, whom I at once for some reason associated with the snow-fairies, were chattering in fluid groups, sailing from one group to another, waving a graceful arm and hallooing across the yard at an indistinguishable crony over in another blue-and-white mirage. And every now and then a flight of nuns tracing a black drift across the yard, and twitters of 'Good morning Mother, good morning Sister' along their trail. Carol and Jessica had made for groups of acquaintances, and I was left up to my own devices. There were other new girls hanging about awkwardly like myself. Soon a bell rang, spreading a last decorous flutter about the yard before it was gracefully sucked into the portals all around.

I was in the same class as Carol, not that this promised to be of the remotest significance. She placed herself in the front row, in the desk that was immediately under the teacher's. I had a feeling that it would be somehow presumptuous of me to sit anywhere but in the back row.

Mrs Wattman, the form mistress, was a stout woman with a faintly apologetic, twitchy manner. She seemed to be uneasy about her dress, or her stoutness, or something about her person – she constantly adjusted her belt and patted her hair. She wore lipstick in a most curious fashion, I thought – it was applied only to a stingy area on either lip, so that from a distance you thought that her mouth ended where the lipstick ended.

A number of the girls in the class were perfectly at home, including Carol who like them had come up through Kindergarten and Lower School at St Ann's. They chattered excitedly among themselves while the new girls sat and watched in awe. Mrs Wattman wanted to know where they had all been for the vacation, and leaned forward to listen with a rapt and doting expression on her face. She giggled helplessly when Carol marched up onto the platform to tell her news illustrated by drawings on the blackboard. Presently Mrs Wattman began to look at her watch and call the class to order. 'No no, one more, one more, Mrs Wattman, I have one more,' protested Carol, doing a little dance and clapping her hands. This continued for some time, and Carol told several more before she consented to come down.

Much of the week was spent in selecting people for various posts, for the choir, the Dramatic Society, the netball team. Sister Benedicta made the whole class sing together and removed some of us after a few bars. The others were further sifted and a number chosen to go into the choir. Carol was among them. It seemed to me that it was more or less the same girls who were picked for the Dramatic Society, but I concluded that it was because singing and acting were related talents. But when many of these same girls were also deemed to be the ones who were sufficiently sporting to be allowed onto the tennis courts, I decided it must be because most of them had come up from Lower School so that their abilities were known to the nuns and teachers, and that the rest of us would have a better chance of being chosen after we had spent some time at St Ann's.

But then Jessica had always been at St Ann's, and she was neither in the choir nor anything else but the Second Company of Guides. I thought perhaps this was why I sometimes saw Auntie Beatrice contemplating her with a kind of anxiety, sizing her up from one angle and then from another, and seeming to shake her head in despair.

Auntie Beatrice was bending all her efforts towards forcing me in as a triplet to Carol and Jessica. She suggested I join the Guides and she seemed exasperated when she asked which company I'd been placed in and I said the Second.

The evening when she announced that she was going to try to get me into Carol's dancing school was a stormy one. Carol pushed her chair back violently and banged on the table: 'She's not coming there!'

Auntie Beatrice did not get many words in, or could not be heard, at any rate. And then some time later she was fanning herself and Carol was storming up the stairs shouting: 'Well you're not going to tell them she's my cousin or anything like that!'

Auntie Beatrice planned to take me along with Carol the next time she had a dancing class, but Carol said she'd rather die, so she stayed away. It was the next Saturday afternoon.

'Remember to speak nicely, dear,' whispered Auntie Beatrice anxiously to me as we went up Miss de Vertueil's steps. We stood in the gallery for a moment. Auntie Beatrice seemed to clear her throat and we went in.

We came into a twittering room full of half-dressed children of all shapes and sizes leaning up against walls and standing about with their legs weirdly twisted. There were squat little ones who rolled here and there like tubs on a pair of stumpy pillars, and tall thin ones with their chins in the air like miniature film stars, and a regrettable number whose proportions could not be likened to anything in particular.

A young lady, also half-dressed, hurried in through one door talking breathlessly and hurried out through another door, still talking breathlessly.

'Miss de Vertueil!' squeaked a pot-bellied child with no bottom, 'someone here to see you!'

I had not realized that anyone had noticed us.

'Thank you, dear,' said Auntie Beatrice, 'that is very nice of you.' The child shot her a faintly contemptuous look. Miss de Vertueil hurried in again, still talking breathlessly. She looked around the room for the visitor.

'Oh, afternoon Mrs McNeil,' she said flatly, and seemed to be ready to hurry off again. Her lipstick was such a bright red that her mouth seemed to be jumping out of her face.

'Afternoon Miss de Vertueil, how are you?'

But Miss de Vertueil was talking again, her back half turned to us. Auntie Beatrice cleared her throat.

'I have my little niece with me,' she said somewhat apologetically. Miss de Vertueil had now taken hold of a nearby child and was twisting its arm and neck here and there like dough.

'Mmm?' she said, busily kneading the child.

'My sister's little girl, you know, the sister I told you Carol takes after.'

'Mmm,' said Miss de Vertueil.

'I was wondering if you could try her out for the troupe.'

Miss de Vertueil now turned her head, saw me, looked behind me, then looked at me again with disbelief.

'Here she is, she is called Cynthia.'

'All right, we'll give her a rhythm test,' said Miss de Vertueil absently.

She went about the room kneading children into bizarre shapes. Then she turned on a record-player and some sleepy music oozed out into the room and all the bodies began to revolve or stretch themselves or dart about; one girl limped heavily from one end of the room to the other while flapping her arms, like a fat hen bent on taking flight. Miss de Vertueil raced about among them talking hurriedly, twisting an arm or a leg into another direction. Then once, when she flitted past where we stood, she became aware of us. 'Go on,' she said in mid-flight, 'dance!' and flitted on her way. Auntie Beatrice more or less pushed me into the whirlpool of bodies wherein I collided with a ballet-dancer spinning for all she was worth with her arms outspread and who, when she could focus me, fixed her face into an expression like a drunk person trying to look superciliously irate.

'Go on, dear,' Auntie Beatrice was urging worriedly, 'dance!'

The fact was that nothing would have been more incongruous and foreign to the circumstances than to dance. What both Miss de Vertueil and Auntie Beatrice meant was that I should promenade about with my feet twisted at unlikely angles, waving my arms about and occasionally reaching towards the ceiling, and this I was permitted to do at any tempo I pleased, for obviously the music was not of any relevance to the proceedings.

I began a half-hearted movement, for Auntie Beatrice looked as if she would burst into tears or start fanning herself if I didn't do something. I felt a complete fool, but would have been a thousand times more embarrassed were it not for the fact that no one was watching, no one but Auntie Beatrice whose head was darting right and left and up and down like a disturbed mother bird. To my relief the music tailed off almost immediately. I rejoined Auntie Beatrice. Miss de Vertueil was nowhere to be seen. Presently she came hurriedly out of a door and went and tended the record-player, then started moving about through the children, talking hurriedly. Then she came past and saw us. She took a step backwards.

'Oh. Mrs McNeil,' she said. 'Oh, awfully sorry, but er – what's her name again?'

'Cynthia,' said Auntie Beatrice, almost toppling towards Miss de Vertueil.

'Oh yes. Awfully sorry but I don't think Cynthia will do. Tried Miss Grieve's troupe?'

'Oh!' shuddered Auntie Beatrice, growing conspiratorial, 'such *or*dinry little children!'

But Miss de Vertueil was half-turned again and she shrugged her shoulders and said something or other with a hurried smile on it before she flitted away again.

Auntie Beatrice said that I would go along with Carol and Jessica to all the birthday parties and garden parties they went to, for I needed to come out among nice people's children. She often lamented the fact that she had not got me when I was little so that I could have gone to Kindergarten like all nice people's children.

And then she was suppressing the clothes I had brought with me: 'Do you really like that dress, dear?' she would suggest to me with a faint turning up of the nose over the broadest of smiles. Some things simply disappeared from the wardrobe to make room for the new clothes. And when one Sunday I appeared for Mass in a dress Tantic had made for me and which was my favourite, Auntie Beatrice threw up her hands in horror and hauled me upstairs to dress me in an outfit of Carol's, discarding the offending garment in a sorry heap on the floor.

'But that is *my* dress!' exclaimed Carol when we rejoined the others.

'Yes I know, darling, but you didn't expect her to go to Mass in that niggery-looking dress, did you?'

'I don't care, that is *my* dress,' pouted Carol, folding her arms in stubbornness. All the way to the church Auntie Beatrice tried to coax her out of her huff. Carol threatened to shame her by doing something wicked in the church. Auntie Beatrice seemed quite frightened by this and pleaded with her in such an abject voice that I felt most unbearably guilty at being the cause of the whole affair. As we were about to enter the church door Auntie Beatrice cast a final pleading, almost tearful look at Carol whose face was still tightened into defiance but who was obviously enjoying herself.

Mass continued to be a strain on my resources. At school I was taking in the catechism pages at a time, and Auntie Beatrice said I was to be christened into the Catholic Church. But for the moment crossing myself and genuflecting and bowing and kneeling and rising and sitting at the appointed cues while keeping track of the stream of murmuring which I was assured was printed in the little book I held in front of me, presented a challenge of the most terrifying order. It was bad enough that Carol and Jessica kept a wicked eye on me while they slid gracefully from one appointed position to another and did not hesitate to giggle into their little books when I shot upwards as the whole congregation lowered itself to its knees. But the whole atmosphere seemed to be one of reproof, of trial; it was as if the whole church, people and building, were coldly regarding me, waiting to pull me up when I fell out of line.

◆

The day of Moonie's wedding approached and there was no mention of it. So on the Friday when I came home from school I hinted bravely to Auntie Beatrice that I would have to go and pack.

'Go and pack?' she said with smiling alarm.

'Yes,' I said, 'for the wedding.'

'Oh, you mean that coolie affair? Look, dear, your aunt is very wrong to drag you along to these things. You have nothing to do in that simmy-dimmy. Tomorrow we'll go for a nice long drive and maybe drop in on your Auntie Beryl – what about

that? I will write and tell your Aunt Rosa that you have the
'flu.'

I nodded and hung my head, for my eyes were filled with
tears of bitter disappointment.

'I know you must miss your little brother, dear, but I'll tell
you what, we'll drive you home next weekend and come for you
on Sunday night.'

I nodded again and fled.

That night I lay awake for hours in a resentment mixed with
apprehension. I thought of the wedding. I thought of Moonie
mysteriously transfigured into a startlingly pretty and fragile
doll smothered in folds of delicate cloth and flowers and surrounded and petted by a drove of women vast and meagre, all
shrouded in uhr'ni; you could never recognize the bride for the
tough young girl you had seen striding past morning and
evening with a pitch-oil tin full of water on her head and a
bucketful in her hand; you could never recognize her afterwards
either, swaying past with a pitch-oil tin of water on her head
and a hefty youngster on her hip.

And the grave young men who could beat the drum like the
devil and did so non-stop until the sharp beat had taken hold of
the night like a hiccup; and the babus in sparkling white dhotis
squatting with their sticks and peering up myopically at the
great crowd.

Toddan would have had his castor-oil by now. Just like at
Christmas, Tantie prepared our insides for similar sprees a week
in advance. I thought of dalpouri and good hot pepper. The
height of festivity to Toddan and me was eating off a piece of
banana-leaf, in the happy event of the supply of plates being
insufficient. Auntie Beatrice had an aversion to hot pepper; she
said it was nastiness. It was never seen in the house. I thought
of Ma's pepper-sauce that was a favourite in Pointe d'Espoir
market. And we poured it over everything – rice, fish-soup, even

bread; and that made her laugh. I suddenly thought with alarm that Auntie Beatrice would find a way of keeping me here even at vacations – *she might not let me go up to Ma*! But no, I remembered with relief, Tantie had said that Auntie Beatrice had no right at all over me, for my father had sent a paper and they had been to court and any day I wanted to leave that bitch's house she couldn't stop me, just write, or if I wanted to come right away I was to phone to Ling and give them the message. That arse Selwyn an'-all, Tantie said, would have to bring God an' He Mother. Tantie said that so very often. I had a brief sleepy vision of Tantie at the front door fighting off my father as she had fought with Mikey the day she'd wanted go and spit on Mrs Hinds. Maybe Tantie would appear tomorrow and do battle with Auntie Beatrice and then haul me off to the wedding, I thought sleepily. When I fell asleep I was thinking of dalpouri and I dreamt that I was the bride and Tantie and Toddan were trying to get through the crowd of shrouded figures surrounding me but in the end they had to give up and go home; without even talking to me.

Auntie Beatrice had said that I would go home for the next weekend. But I knew that on Saturday was one of the next-door children's birthday party.

17

For all of Auntie Beatrice's efforts Carol and Jessica had no intention whatsoever of letting me into their dubious confrèrie. There was no love lost between them, but nothing could unite them like a conspiracy of giggling immediately behind my back.

As for Bernadette, well Bernadette did not seem to have established my existence at all, so that it could hardly be said that she ignored me. She came and went, with fantastically piled hairdos, dangerously high thin heels, and a most unlikely affectedness in her speech. She spent hours on the telephone, when her voice would arch through the house: '. . . so well I said well dorling why don't we just go and pick the others up orfterwards . . . .'

On weekends her cronies filled the gallery, chatting, playing records, flirting. One Sunday afternoon we triplets were decked out and sent to the cinema; our social life was the full-time occupation of Auntie Beatrice, and the walk to Regal, down Harris street, along one side of the Park and then the length of St Cyr Boulevard better known as San-See, was an approved fashion-parade promenade for those who cared to avail themselves of it.

The three of us had to pass through the gallery where Bernadette's crowd was in session. As we walked down the front path one of the exaggeratedly feminine voices of the assembly floated down to us.

'But which is which, Bernie? I can never remember their names.' And Bernadette's off-hand voice replied: 'Oh the nice one is Carol, the fairskin' one; and the other one is Jessica.'

'But who is the third one, then?'

'Oh that's some lil relative Mommer found up in the country.'

But beginning to be quite as redoubtable as their contempt was Auntie Beatrice's attention. I squirmed under her benignancy. There was no reason why her face should open out into a smile whenever she laid eyes on me, or why she should smile continuously while talking to me whatever the nature of the statement.

It was not an unpleasant smile. It reminded me of a picture of my mother that Tantie sometimes showed to us. Auntie Beatrice otherwise constantly evoked my 'poor mother' and seemed to think that I remembered every detail about her person and had never ceased to mourn her loss.

I took it for granted at first that my mother was a poor soul because she'd had the misfortune to die. But bit by bit I gathered that a misfortune quite as regrettable had overtaken her while still living.

The large oval photograph, reddish-brown with age and encircled in a heavy frame of gilded foliage, that hung high up on the wall and leaned over into the attention of all who entered the livingroom, was that of The White Ancestress, Elizabeth Helen Carter. The photograph was as faded as a photograph could manage to be, but Auntie Beatrice said that the minute Carol came into the world everybody could see that she resembled her, and so Carol's middle name was Elizabeth, as my poor mother was also named.

Elizabeth Carter was really the last ancestor worthy of mention, for after her things went from bad to worse. Auntie Beatrice thought it necessary to excuse my mother's own misdemeanour to me. It wasn't really her fault, she was a grown girl after all, and as such she couldn't stay on the Godparents' hands much longer – she'd taken almost the first comer. And up there in the bush there wasn't anything that was her quality, really. 'If it hadn't been for him,' she reflected mournfully, 'you might have looked like her.'

It was the Godparents' fault, too, they were low-class people and had no idea about anything. Elizabeth was *such* a beautiful little girl that when the family had had to go all ways the people up on The Grange had been willing to have her, and they would even have taken her back to England with them – Auntie Beatrice sighed heavily here after the sheer effort of conceiving of such a thing – but she went to the Godparents, she who by right belonged with the people up on The Grange, and look what had happened.

I began to have the impression that I should be thoroughly ashamed; for it seemed to me that my person must represent the rock-bottom of the family's fall from grace. Sometimes when I was alone in the living-room Elizabeth Carter's indistinguishable portrait grew features, a pair of eyes that frowned angrily and a mouth that was pursed together with disapproval.

18

Uncle Norman struck me as having, at some previous date, retreated permanently before Auntie Beatrice's tireless initiative and talkativeness; or before the unbelievable propensity to rioting that engaged the rest of the household. Most of the time he was either absent or unnoticeable. When he was at home he spent a great deal of time outside doing something unspecified to the car.

Auntie Beatrice seemed mostly to resign herself to his abdication, even to be quite in favour of it. But she was often to be heard calling upon him in a reproachful voice out of the depths of a riot, or when one of the three had gone out of their way to kick her in her teeth. Then it was mainly his fault that things were as they were in that family. In particular, Auntie Beatrice seemed to blame Jessica on Uncle Norman.

'I really don't know what to do with Jessica, you know, Norman, this child has no ambition at all!'

Uncle Norman nodded vaguely, and this inflamed Auntie Beatrice.

'And you are not any damn help, yourself! How can I bring up this family when you never say anything?'

'Mm. You say enough for all of us,' commented Uncle Norman without interrupting his leisurely feeding. Auntie Beatrice threw her hands up and rolled her eyes heavenward, and in frustration fell upon Jessica again. Jessica, who very often came in for this kind of public trial at meal-times, began to jab dismally at her food.

'It's not my fault, I tell you Sister Columba don' like me.'

'Sister Columba *doesn't* . . .!' barked Auntie Beatrice.

'Oh I know it's doesn't, give me a chance, nuh!'

'Well then *say* doesn't! If you want to talk like any old ordnry market-people then you can go and live with market-people!'

'And they only pick the fair girls anyway. . . .'

'Look, my girl, it's not any fault of mine that you are dark; you just have to take one look at me and you will see that! There you have nothing to reproach *me* for. But the darker you are the harder you have to try, I am tired of telling you that! What you don't have in looks you have to make up for otherwise!'

Uncle Norman eyed her mildly.

I grew very uneasy whenever Auntie Beatrice spoke harshly to anyone. It made her unwearying kindness to me seem all the more unbearable and precarious. Her smile was now to me like when we used to dare each other to look straight up into the sun. The most violent of Tantie's rampages would now have been a *comfortable* experience, somehow, compared to Auntie Beatrice's smilingness which made my toes curl with shyness. Sir lashing out with his tamarind whip used to inspire in me a faint urge to giggle into his face. But Auntie Beatrice I could not cope with. She was a perpetual assault on me before which I recoiled.

I did not want to be *put* to bed night after night, with a figure bending over me in the half-light and talking in a whisper while

92

I lay stiff with agony at the thought that at any moment the face was going to descend with a kiss.

And I could manage my own hair, admirably, in fact, Tantie thought – it had been some time since she had stopped combing it for me; she only did so when we were dressing up, or sometimes just 'for sweetness'. Auntie Beatrice had no right to take possesion of my head every morning, even going so far as to tie my bows. I submitted to this, however great my distaste, for with Auntie Beatrice I was disarmed beyond all resistance, in an uncomfortable, alien way. It was all I could do to slink into the bathroom every time and there angrily untie and retie my bows.

Carol and Jessica quite simply did not allow Auntie Beatrice near their hair. And while she combed my hair on mornings she carried on a monologue for the benefit of these two.

'*Some* children think they are too grown-up; some children think they fell out of the sky, you know, Cynthia, some children think they have no use whatsoever for anybody but themselves; but never mind, they soon find that they are not needed either. Here is a child who knows what it is to be a child.'

The two ignored her studiously as they went about their business of getting ready for school. My discomfort was complete, in a situation which repeated itself under one form or another almost every day. At the table the others sat where they felt like sitting, but Auntie Beatrice kept me firmly in place next to her, and at the height of battle with Bernadette, or Carol, or all three combined, she reached for me and drew me to her, while she fanned herself distractedly with her other hand.

Since the weekend of Moonie's wedding neither Auntie Beatrice nor I had brought up the subject of my going home for a weekend. Auntie Beatrice had never once mentioned Tantie's name since, though I often thought she was close to it as when she spoke bitterly of what had become of poor little Elizabeth because her low-class Godparents had got her and not the people up on The Grange; and often when we two were alone in the kitchen (Auntie Beatrice was unable, by threats or by plaintiveness, to recruit the help of the others in the kitchen) and she had stopped talking for a few minutes, so that she realized that I was silent, she would suddenly ask with apprehension what it was I was thinking about.

As for me, I was no more disposed to broaching the subject than she was, at first out of sheer pusillanimity, and then later because day by day it had grown more unthinkable.

Carnival came, and I discovered that I did not even want to go home for Carnival. We went to the Stands on both days, where we sat primly and watched the bands in the company of the tourists and of the nice people who were in two minds about Carnival – saw the unmistakable niggeryness of the affair (real nigger-break-loose, said Bernadette) but were not able either to stay at home and extract themselves from it. Bernadette was the only one in the house who was playing mas', because through Roger Hemandez she could get into Starpoints. Of course Carol could get into Starpoints too, said Auntie Beatrice, but maybe next year. We were to look out for Bernadette to wave to her, and we spotted her easily as the band came by tripping and orderly.

And sitting wedged against an American tourist, he in a hot shirt of many colours, Bermuda shorts of many other colours and a broad panama hat with a polka-dot band, we in our sober and tasteful jeans and jerseys, I remembered in a flash of embarrassment Ramlaal's inelegant truck into which we used to pile with a herd of neighbours and neighbours' children for the trip to Coriaca to see Carnival there. The ride was a rollicking one; often the truck stalled from sheer overweight and then half the load would jump off and push and then jump on again whereupon the truck would promptly shudder to a halt once more. We sang all the way and drummed on our chocolate and pitch-oil tins that contained the pelau and roti and dalpouri and chicken. It had always been an event we looked forward to even more than Christmas. One year we had all four played mas' – Toddan and Mikey played djab'-djab' and Mikey carried Toddan on his shoulders, letting him down when they stopped to do their accosting act. Toddan had danced, gravely, fatly, his round belly doing an extra quiver at each strut, and clapping, delighted crowds had gathered around him. The two of them had collected a sum of money that seemed to Toddan and me a fortune.

All this I was seeing again through a kind of haze of shame; and I reflected that even now Tantie and Toddan must be packed into that ridiculous truck with all those common raucous niggery people and all those coolies.

◆

And then the Easter vacation was approaching, and Auntie Beatrice took it for granted that I was coming with them to Canapo, where they were renting a beach-house. She had not spoken of writing to Tantie to tell her, but I knew that I would have to write, anyway, unless I wanted to see Tantie appear at Auntie Beatrice's front door to tell her what was what, the thought of which gave me an unpleasant shiver.

So I wrote to Tantie, telling her that I was going to spend the holidays down at Canapo, that I wanted to because I had never been down there before.

19

We arrived at Canapo in brooding weather. The sky hung low all around us and the sea was dark and forbidding. Cosy Nook, as the house called itself, lay in a cove shut in on one side by a rising finger of land jutting out into the sea, known as The Head. The cove was filled in with the same dense dark green fury as crowded down the steep slope of The Head, greenness like Ma's land.

The house was not large, and I decided on the first day that I would not be spending a great deal of time indoors.

Uncle Norman slept for most of the time. He said that vacations were not made for striding up and down beaches and soaking yourself in salt water, and that for his part he could have spent *his* vacation right there in town. Auntie Beatrice sighed. She despaired of inculcating in him the ways of nice people.

We went down to the beach together on the first day and on the second day. But on the third day the Silvas suddenly appeared on the scene. They were staying in a beach-house on the other side of The Head. At first Auntie Beatrice watched in beaming satisfaction while Bernadette and Carol and Jessica paraded the beach, mingled with them and only slightly distinguishable from the da Silva boys and girls and the other youngsters they had brought with them (the da Silvas and their friends had been there for a week, sunbathing). But then they started disappearing from the house on mornings without even sitting down to breakfast, and then Auntie Beatrice was deprived even of the joy of watching the crowd, for they went with them over to the other side of The Head, where they said the water was better.

I was very sorry for Auntie Beatrice. She watched them go without a word of protest. They left noisily in their bright beach-clothes, promising to be back for lunch, and Auntie Beatrice seemed to shrug her shoulders as the gay noise died away into the coconut trees. Then the walls closed in on the two of us; Uncle Norman was usually asleep when they left and we didn't go down to the beach before he was up. I wanted quite simply to flee, but I was most abjectly sorry for Auntie Beatrice. And in any case she was not prepared to let me out of sight. Once when I disappeared into the toilet she went about the house calling frantically after me, and shut into the tiny room I had a moment of unreasonable, fluttering panic – I was afraid to answer, and for a few wild seconds even envisaged clambering up to the high window.

We ate breakfast together, the two of us, with Auntie Beatrice refilling my cup every time I had taken two sips from it and inspecting my face with anxiety whenever I refused more food. Then we washed up together. Auntie Beatrice talked in a dejected stream, reminding me what a good child I was, and she was sure I'd never treated my poor mother like that. We tidied the house, and then we went and stood leaning over the bannister of the gallery, staring out at the sea, until Uncle Norman woke up.

One morning I made up my mind to run away. Auntie Beatrice would have to wait by herself until Uncle Norman woke up. While the others made their deafening exit through the front door I scuttled through the back door and sped across the yard, making for the bushes at the side of the house. I had barely plunged into the thick shrubbery when I began to hear Auntie Beatrice's voice calling me. The desperation in her voice grew and I fought my way wildly through the bushes; I was

97

being mercilessly scratched and bruised, but I had to escape the sound of her voice. When I got to the other side I could still hear her calling, almost hysterically, and I thought she must be out in the backyard. I ran for all I was worth, towards the beach; when I got to more sandy ground it was more difficult to make progress, my feet sank in and seemed to slide back at each step, and a cold fear washed over me, I thought that at any moment Auntie Beatrice's hand would descend on my shoulder from behind, and that I would collapse onto the sand in terror and remorse.

I was still running, but I would have to rest soon. I thought of the growth of vines that fringed the beach in places, and the little alcoves they formed. There I could hide.

◆

I sat curled into a thicket. The vines grew along a little shelf that rose up from the beach, and I looked out over the bay. Over on the other side I could make out the three moving along The Head. At once I shut out the thought of Auntie Beatrice, and tried to think of something else. The beach at Pointe d'Espoir and all the cousins and Godsisters and Godbrothers. That was another thought to shut out, for suddenly I saw us coming up out of the water with our petticoats and panties and old trousers clutching at our bodies, and some of us who hadn't bothered to find a piece of tattered clothing to bathe in, naked. And then Ma. Ma who sold in the market. Ma who was a market-woman. I wondered if Auntie Beatrice were aware of this fact. Then I thought with bottomless horror *suppose Bernadette and Carol and Jessica came to know of this*! It was not a thought to linger upon for one second. Frantically I swept it out of my mind, and into the vacuum floated Auntie Beatrice, leaning on the bannister, looking out to sea, as I was crouching there looking out at the sea.

I was irritated at the sea. I considered it had no right to roll itself to and fro, to and fro, in such a satisfied manner, as though nothing at all was wrong. And the sea-birds and the jumbled footprints in the sand and the dead leaves insulted me, too.

After some time I decided to go home. There was nothing to be done and besides Uncle Norman must be awake by now. I crawled out and made my way along the beach, staying up where the sand was dry, for it was dry sand that impeded your footsteps.

Auntie Beatrice managed to sink a smile into her consternation: 'Where were you, dear?'

'I went for a walk.'

'But why didn't you say?'

'I said I was going . . . maybe you didn't hear.'

She eyed me curiously, the smile bravely in place.

'I wanted you to come down to the village with me, to get some things for tonight.'

Auntie Beatrice had been coaxing the others to bring the da Silvas and their friends home. They were coming that evening. We spent the morning down on the beach, and in the afternoon Auntie Beatrice prevailed upon Uncle Norman to drive us not to the village but to the nearest town, ten miles away. But he made it clear that once we'd got there he was going to find a nice big tree to park under and he was going to sleep and we could go and lose ourselves in the town if we wanted to.

We did a prodigious amount of shopping. I hung a few feet behind Auntie Beatrice, and whenever I could help it, did not go into the shops with her. For Auntie Beatrice made a systematic effort not to understand a word of what the shop-people said to her, and when she spoke to them it was loudly, slowly and emphatically, with much pointing and sign-language. I found this most painful, especially after one shopkeeper remarked under his breath to the rest of his amused clients: 'I wonder whe' this one come-out, boy? Mus' be land yesterday!

Ma'am, take mih picture,
An' I sing a kaiso for you!'

And Auntie Beatrice went from shop to shop complaining that there was no proper food to be got down here in this bush, barely a bottle of stuffed olives and a bag of potato crisps and as for things like Worcester sauce and French dressing well it was a good thing we'd brought our own supply of food that was all she could say. Nevertheless we managed to reach the car laden. We had bought enough food and drinks to keep more than the da Silvas and their friends happy for a whole evening.

We spent the rest of the day in the kitchen, preparing the spread. Auntie Beatrice fairly skipped about the kitchen humming to herself like a little girl. When dusk began to fall she sent me out every few minutes to see if they were coming. Every few minutes she stopped her feverish activity and cocked her ear.

Then there were voices coming into the yard. Auntie Beatrice broke into an excited smile, wiped her hands vigorously and hung up her apron. She looked into a mirror and patted her hair before sailing out of the kitchen. I stayed in the kitchen. I had no intention of coming out until it was absolutely necessary.

I heard talking in the gallery, and after a while the talking was coming through the house towards the kitchen. Then my heart sank, for Auntie Beatrice seemed to be pleading. Then Bernadette said something in an irritated voice about the moon, and that they hadn't known. I felt a wave of nameless desolation. Then Auntie Beatrice's voice came into full earshot: 'But they could still have come to dinner, and you could have gone afterwards!'

'All right, all right,' said Bernadette, as she came into the kitchen and made for the stove, 'what do you want me to do, go over there and call them?'

She lifted the lids off the saucepans and peeped in and sniffed, before fetching herself a plate. Carol and Jessica came in and followed suit.

I slunk out of the kitchen. I went and sat in the gallery. I observed that the sea was still offensively rolling itself backwards and forwards; no respect, no respect for anything whatsoever. Suppose I were to drown here at Canapo. Tomorrow, maybe. It was the first agreeable thought I'd had for the day.

After a while I went in again. It wouldn't do to be sitting there when the others came through. So I decided to go and lie on my bed until they had gone. As I entered the bedroom, before my eyes had got used to the dimness, a form rose from one of the beds, making my heart stop.

'Go and eat, darling,' said Auntie Beatrice, and sank onto the bed again. I retreated, stumbling, and went back out into the gallery. But I couldn't stay in the gallery either, so where could I go?

I crept out, stole around the house, and took refuge in the bushes. At once I was assailed by a screaming cloud of mosquitoes and sand-flies, and frantically tore off a branch with which I threshed the air and bushes while keeping up a contortion of slapping and scratching; but here I stayed until I could hear the others leaving. Then I crept into the house again. Auntie Beatrice was still lying down, and I had no appetite whatsoever, so I sat down in the gallery again.

I started violently when she came shuffling out. She sat down.

'Well, it's just the two of us again,' she said with a wrinkled smile. I looked elsewhere.

'Do you know where my daughters are?' she said, looking out to sea, so that I did not think it necessary to make any kind of replying sound, 'they have gone *crab*-hunting, if you please.'

She seemed to laugh somewhere down in her belly.

'Bernadette screams like a madwoman when she sees a little baby spider.'

I remembered that Ma's bigger boys used to go off gleefully with crocus-bags and flash-lights and lengths of vine when it was full moon, and Ma didn't think it fitting that girls and small children be caught straying along the beach after nightfall.

We sat in silence, until Uncle Norman emerged and asked where all the company was. Auntie Beatrice shot a resentful glance at him then got up and went in. Uncle Norman scratched the back of his head. Then he asked me what had happened and I told him.

The three of us ate dinner with the sumptuous array spread obscenely around us. After we'd eaten Auntie Beatrice laid dishcloths over everything, the sandwiches, the nuts, olives and fancy biscuits. Then she said we were going for a walk, she and I.

We walked along the beach in the direction of The Head. I appreciated the silence. It meant that Auntie Beatrice's thoughts were elsewhere, so that I was safe.

When she began to talk she did not stop. She said it was so sad when a family could not be a family. When she was little they'd had to go and live all in different places when their father left their mother, and she'd always dreamt of them coming to live in the same house again. And when that never happened she'd dreamt of having her own family.

'Hm!' she laughed shortly. 'You see the family I got! Spend my life teaching my children to be decent, teaching them what is important, and then they forget who it was that got them where they are.'

She said what a good child I was and it was God's will after all that my poor mother should die, all things were for the best, for now she had a comfort. Then she drew in her breath, and asked me in a voice as if it were something else she had wanted to ask me: 'What do you think your aunt and your little brother are doing now?'

102

I said I did not know, and this reply seemed to satisfy her, for then she began to talk about something else. Then suddenly she broke off and said rapidly: 'Do you still want to go and see your aunt.'

This struck into the heart of my confusion. But I resolved that whatever my real thoughts, I owed it to Tantie to make a show of loyalty before Auntie Beatrice. So I replied, thankful of the dark, yes.

Auntie Beatrice's step seemed to quicken, and before long she had started talking again, about something else. We were walking along The Head, and its dark mass seemed to be leaning over us.

As we approached the end of The Head the sea grew noisy where it swirled about the black clump of rocks. Suddenly there was a confusion of excited voices coming from the other side and then dark forms and bobbing round lights burst around the point. They stopped and all seemed to be looking downwards. Something small glided into a pale circle on the sand and then stopped abruptly in its tracks. The crab drew in its eyes and crouched down with its legs curled under, and one of the forms sprang forward, deftly took hold of it and popped it into a crocus-bag.

The whole length of the other side of The Head was alive with excited voices and lights flitting about like large candle-flies. Auntie Beatrice had stopped talking, and I walked along fascinated and strangely affected by the half-lit excitement and the yellow beams that transfixed these swift creatures onto the sand. The sea air was a little chilly.

We were approaching a group of lights coming towards us, and I was following their progress with a kind of unwilling anticipation. I must have forgotten that I was walking beside Auntie Beatrice, but that could not have been. I do not think that I forgot Auntie Beatrice for one moment.

Perhaps I had been walking straight into the group, and she had only wanted to draw me aside, out of their way. We had come within a few yards of them. They were chasing a crab and then it was trapped in the glare. It was when a boy sprang forward to take it that the hand took hold of mine and I savagely slapped the hand away and recoiled and turning sharply I was staring helplessly into Auntie Beatrice's face. It was only a ragged, dirtyish light that lay on her features, but I wished that it were pitch dark so that I would never have seen the devastation in her eyes and around her mouth.

After a few more steps Auntie Beatrice said it was getting late, and we turned and made our way home, rather hurriedly and in absolute silence.

20

The next morning after the others had disappeared Auntie Beatrice said to me without looking at me that I could go for a walk if I wanted to and I didn't really have to stay in the house. I did not quite know how to take this, so I hung about in some discomfort. She started to set the house in order and when I went and fetched a broom to sweep as usual she took it away from me and said that we would not be eating breakfast before Uncle Norman got up.

There was nothing to do but go. And so it was every day for the remaining time at Canapo: pointedly and reproachfully Auntie Beatrice left me to my own devices. The smile did not vanish altogether, and our camaraderie remained almost intact when the other three were about, but I knew that the air had changed. Everything seemed to be a different colour from before. The Head was a monstrous enemy, it was in cahoots with the sea.

◆

The vacation ended and we came home again. The house at Canapo had been small, but there had been my vine alcove where I could spend hours of cramped safety. Now there was no escaping. Every movement I made seemed to provoke some deadly imminent fate to fall in upon me. Auntie Beatrice seemed to me to be biding her time.

At midday when we came home from school we helped ourselves to lunch out of the pots and pans. One day I absent-mindedly put my food into a bowl and took a dessert-spoon with which to eat it. The other two stared, their forks suspended in the air, and then looked at each other and burst out giggling. Carol went and called Auntie Beatrice who came rushing in with an expression almost of grim satisfaction on her face.

'What's the matter, Cynthia, weren't there any more plates and knives and forks?'

'Yes,' I replied lamely, aware now of the nature of my transgression but deeply puzzled nevertheless; I merely found it very comfortable to eat rice out of a bowl and with a spoon instead of chasing it all over a plate with a fork.

'Well just you *find* them for me please!' she ordered with a vehemence that startled me. 'Don't bring your ordryness here! *We* don't eat with bowl and spoon here, you're not living at your precious *Tantie* now!'

From then on it was a steep slope downhill. Auntie Beatrice announced her firm intention to haul me out of what she termed alternately my ordinaryness and my niggeryness. Tantie, referred to as 'that woman,' now received her full share of blame for this state of affairs, to think that the woman should believe she had the right, and what will happen to the boy, what will happen to him? God will prove me right he will turn into a worthless little vagabond, that is what will happen to him, what can that woman teach him, a woman with no culture, no breeding, no sense of right and wrong herself, what can she teach the child, I will live to see him spurn that woman and blush at her name, mark my words.

Bernadette had by now unfortunately ceased to ignore me; she began to be thoroughly irritated by my presence. Almost every time she laid eyes on me she would tell me to go and powder my greasy face and she didn't know how I managed to be so greasy-looking all the time like a stevedore. And she shooed me unceremoniously out of the drawingroom whenever any of her friends came. Above all when Roger Hernandez came.

But it must be said in all fairness that everyone was shooed out of sight when Roger came, even Carol. Auntie Beatrice bundled us out into the kitchen to finish eating, for example, if Roger happened to drop by in the middle of dinner.

Auntie Beatrice took a most lively interest in Bernadette's friends. 'I don't know who that Joseph boy's parents are, Bernadette, you know anything about them, Norman?' and with barely a pause to accommodate Uncle Norman's faint flicker of the eyebrows by way of response: 'Mind you, he's not too bad-looking; he's got a streak of Chinese or something in him, not so?'

'I don't know,' replied Bernadette with irritation, 'he came with David, I don't really know much about him.'

'I see Roger is sporting side-burns nowadays,' prodded Auntie Beatrice, in a voice full of pride.

'So what?' snapped Bernadette. Auntie Beatrice winced visibly and swallowed.

Mrs Harper, who ironed the clothes as violently as if she would have liked to have been doing as much to the wearer of each garment, had a most profound aversion for Roger. When Roger strode through the house to the pantry to fling open the fridge as was his wont and help himself to a drink, the one thing that could make him recoil was Mrs Harper's features curled into a sneer as if there were a bad smell about, and as he departed in haste with his habitual smirk in disarray Mrs Harper muttered about the lil 'Pañol prostitute down in the Place-Sainte who had a chile o' every breed God make and couldn' tell yu which Yankee sailorman she make that pissin'-tail runt for – what these people wouldn' scrape-up outa the rubbish-truck to sharpen they gran'-chirren nose, eh!

21

I wanted to shrink, to disappear. Sometimes I thought I would gladly live under the back steps with Dash, rather than cross their paths all day long. I felt that the very sight of me was an affront to common decency. I wished that my body could shrivel up and fall away, that I could step out new and acceptable.

At times I resented Tantie bitterly for not having let Auntie Beatrice get us in the first place and bring us up properly. What Auntie Beatrice said so often was quite true: how could a woman with no sense of right and wrong take it upon herself to bring up children, God knew the reason why He hadn't given her any of her own. And I was ashamed and distressed to find myself thinking of Tantie in this way.

At school, Mrs Wattman seemed to regard a section of us as

rather a nuisance, marring the décor of the classroom. On mornings and afternoons before the bell rang there was always a huddle of girls around her table, among them Carol, in the midst of which Mrs Wattman sat radiant with pleasure and seemed irritated when the bell rang and the cluster had to disperse and she had to contemplate the rest of us.

With Mrs Wattman Carol always considered herself to be at the centre of the proceedings, and Mrs Wattman looked on at her capers with imbecilic indulgence. Whenever I made so bold as to raise my hand to pose a question Mrs Wattman knitted her brow with exasperation. She had us for History, and I was given up as a hopeless case, as thick-skulled as was to be expected, whenever she pounced on me with a question which I could not answer rapidly, although my place in the class was never lower than third. Carol's academic position wavered between twelfth and twenty-fifth.

Two new girls joined the class in the middle of the term. This was strange, for it was generally known that at the beginning of the year the pupils of the First Forms represented one-tenth of all the applicants. 'I bet you find it horrible and hot down here, eh?' Mrs Wattman oozed on their first day, 'we must let you sit together as you are sisters – who would like to change so Heather and Margaret can sit together?'

As it happened I was one of the noble volunteers, but only because Mrs Wattman looked fixedly at me until I put up my hand.

One afternoon as I sat in Mrs Wattman's History class, bored, I began quite idly and unconsciously to run my ruler backwards and forwards along the partition. Presently a girl came in from the class next door and related something to Mrs Wattman, then turning, pointed to the back corner of the classroom where I sat; Mrs Wattman's head jerked sharply in that direction and she fixed me with a gaze of the most devastating contempt.

108

'Perhaps you think it's funny to sit there and disturb the class next door!'

All eyes were trained on me with curiosity, for no one, least of all myself until it dawned upon me, knew what it was all about; she continued to scorch me with her look, shaking her head slowly. Then in the attentive silence Mrs Wattman delivered her verdict with crushing slowness: 'You are one of those who will never get very far.'

22

I spent a great deal of time sitting on the back steps. I could sit there for hours without anyone missing me. From there I could see across the neighbour's yard over into Harris Street. It was only a short strip of about three yards between the two neighbours' houses. I could see the far pavement, but on the near side I only saw heads bobbing along the top of the high fence. Children took six steps across the strip of pavement. Fat women laboured into sight and were visible for rather a long time. Prim women with high-heeled shoes seemed to take a hundred little clickety steps but they were gone in a flash. Men strode across in three or four noiseless paces but many of them slouched aimlessly over.

At about five o'clock the gap was always full of people. Heads travelling hurriedly in opposite directions along the top of the fence seemed to be on their way to colliding but at the last moment glided miraculously past each other. They were all people who were making their way home, unfalteringly, without dragging their feet, without even thinking which way their home lay and what their home was like, and they would unlatch their front gates and walk up their front paths without even noticing their front gardens or the fronts of their houses and they would be opening their front doors, even, still without a thought for what would be greeting them when they got inside. They were very enviable people. To think that I had once been like them, making my way home day after day without my feet thinking where they were taking me. That seemed to have been a long time ago. It seemed almost never to have happened. If only it *had* never happened. If I had never lived there, if Auntie Beatrice had whisked us away from the very beginning and brought us here, then I would have been nice. I would have been one of them and I would have come home every day just as unthinkingly as Carol and Jessica and the front door would not have been forbidding nor the armchairs in the livingroom disapproving.

The gap cleared again. Now and then a figure wandered across the pavement or a round head bobbed along the top of the fence. Later the street lights came on. Street lights were uncanny. They burst out so suddenly that you expected to hear a sound but there was no sound whatsoever. And in that moment when they sprouted forth they were alive, just for that fraction of a second, but just as abruptly they froze fast. Far over on the other side the Morilla Hills were a smoky colour, beginning to be pierced all over by little slivers of light. And then it was dark, and the evening was a dark blue chamber I was sitting in, bounded by the street and the neighbours' houses and the door behind me, and the sky had lowered itself silently.

For all the sounds around me were suddenly intimate, like urgent whispering. Dash every now and then growling to himself when other dogs barked; the boy's voice thudding cosily about the darkened yard on the other side of the fence. To think that I could envy him for one moment!

110

There ought to be a law, said Auntie Beatrice, people like that living up against decent people, something should be done. Carol and the others referred to the boy as 'Molasses' when they did refer to him, but they did not give him very much thought. Auntie Beatrice willed Divine Judgement, or an epidemic, or simple eviction, upon the boy and his mother and the shifting population of undefinable relatives who inhabited the house.

She had abolished them to some extent by hanging oqaque blue curtains in all the windows along the left side of our house. But one day Mrs Harper calmly parted the kitchen curtains and stood talking comfortably out of the window, now and then producing her dry rumble of a laugh that came from somewhere between her bosom and her belly, in answer to the familiar screaming cackle with the helpless 'Wo-ya! wo-ya!' from across the fence. Auntie Beatrice was in the drawingroom. She sat bolt upright and stared into space with dazed, horror-stricken eyes.

When Mrs Harper had finished talking she said 'Right, mih child,' and a little later the iron could be heard vehemently stabbing the clothes again.

Mrs Harper did the ironing and lumbered through the drawingroom at her processional pace, like a bishop on tour, murmuring curtly as usual: 'I gone.' This always caused deep offence to Auntie Beatrice. She never failed to bid Mrs Harper farewell with a smile and a pleasantness that were as high-pitched as when she talked to the lady on the other side of the fence; but when Mrs Harper had made her way down the path and up the road (Auntie Beatrice peeped out of the window after her) then she would begin again to swear that she would teach that woman to address her in a fitting manner and not to talk to her as if it were a chair she were talking to, she had a name, after all, and in any case she was used to being addressed as 'Madam' by people who worked for her and she had never *known* such disrespect.

Often when there was something Auntie Beatrice had to say to Mrs Harper she came up behind her as she stood at the ironing-table and managed to begin by saying with some sternness 'Mrs Harper!' Mrs Harper took time to settle the iron comfortably, planted a plump hand upon her hip as she slowly revolved, and after she had unhurriedly focused Auntie Beatrice, without moving her lips or any part of her face emitted a brief and uninviting 'Yeas?' Auntie Beatrice's sternness rolled back down her throat and her apologetic smile came on.

That day, as Mrs Harper left, Auntie Beatrice smiled to her with all her might and said 'Goodbye, Mrs Harper,' as usual. But when Mrs Harper was well up the road Auntie Beatrice's offended-and-outraged voice flew out and swore that this was the limit, this was the limit, her patience was tried to the limit not a foot will that woman put in this house again she will be greeted at the door with a pay-envelope and turned away again just let her show herself here next Saturday not a foot will she put in my gallery God be my witness it'll be right about turn and up the road again.

All that week Auntie Beatrice passionately rehearsed Mrs Harper's dismissal, before God who was her witness, before Uncle Norman who by Wednesday was saying that if he heard Mrs Harper's name once more he was going to go and live at his mother's until after Saturday, lengthily and dramatically over the phone and to people who came visiting. By Saturday lunch-time Mrs Harper was going to be greeted at the gate, which would be firmly locked moreover, the pay-envelope was not at all a certainty, and what was more she was going to be told a thing or two before she was sent packing.

Auntie Beatrice was upstairs when Mrs Harper appeared at the gate two hours later. Mrs Harper laboured up the front

steps and was panting through the house and there w
sign of Auntie Beatrice. 'Evenin', child,' she said to m
final, closed-mouth way that always sounded like reproof.

She pounded her way through the bundle of clothes, sometimes muttering disgustedly to herself or cheupsing. She had
nearly finished and Auntie Beatrice had not yet come down.

'Child,' she said suddenly, 'where's yu Auntie.'

'Upstairs.'

She put the iron down loudly.

'But a-a. I say the woman gone-out! Just you go up-there and
ask her for me if she forget is pay-day and if she think I must
come-up there and beg for mih money. A-a!'

I crawled up the steps as though they were a steep mountain-
side and my feet made of lead. I knocked timidly on Auntie
Beatrice's door. There was no answer.

'Auntie Beatrice,' I said to the door, 'Mrs Harper would like
to talk to you.'

The floorboards creaked and then the door came open. Auntie
Beatrice stood glowering at me, holding out an envelope. *→ weak-*
even w/her
'Here,' she said, 'give this to her.' then she shut the door. Mrs *children*
Harper was still doing our ironing, and almost every Saturday
she stood at the kitchen window, or even at the fence, and
chattered with the boy's mother.

◆

Now figures came into the gap with their shadows a dark streak
of oil that their feet were sucking along after them. As they
passed under the street light the oil raced to the front and now
it was gliding along effortlessly pulling the figure behind it. I
knew that all the way along the street it would be playing this
little game; every time the figure approached a street light the
shadow would move to the rear as if it were shy of the light, but

when they got under the light it would cheekily dart to the front again, as if to say 'Catch me if you can!'

Before, I used to help Auntie Beatrice in the kitchen on evenings. But after the holidays she had said sharply that the servant would certainly manage alone, and nobody could say that Beatrice McNeil had taken her sister's child to make a housemaid out of her. So I did not come in from the back steps until dinner time. It was a question of remaining invisible for as great a part of the time as was possible.

I was afraid of one thing more than anything else in the world. Sooner or later Auntie Beatrice would be so tired of the sight of me that she would send me back to Tantie.

◆

One evening when I came in Auntie Beatrice was clearing the table. She looked up at me and went on stacking dishes, more busily than before. She bore the pile of plates out into the kitchen and came briskly in again. As she began to stack more things she said as if to no one in particular (which was almost the only way she ever addressed me now): 'Plenty of food in the kitchen, if our food is good enough for the lady.'

And she whisked out again. Bernadette was on the phone, Carol and Jessica were sprawled or sunk into armchairs with books. They raised one curious eyelid, then went on reading.

For a long moment I stood, at an utter loss. Then timorously I went towards the kitchen where Auntie Beatrice was washing up. I almost knocked, although the door stood wide open. I felt hopelessly in the wrong. I was a burglar creeping over to the cupboard, surreptitiously lifting a plate out and then uncovering and helping myself to food, now and then causing an offensive clank.

I sat and ate awkwardly, almost fearing to chew, stiff with the

114

effort of keeping the knife and fork from making the slightest sound against the plate. Auntie Beatrice stood at the sink, her back to me. So far she had not once turned her head, but I felt as if she were following every movement I made. I wished that she would simply start throwing plates at me. I thought that I would eat hurriedly and slink off. But then what about when I would have to rise from the chair, walk across the floor with outrageously audible footsteps, and, the most dreadful moment of all, put my soiled plate into the sink where Auntie Beatrice was washing up reproachfully alone? No remark that she was then likely to make could be more distasteful to me than my own gesture of lowering the plate which I had dirtied into a sink already full of what Auntie Beatrice termed 'work for the donkey'. So I began to eat more slowly, so that she would be done before I had finished, and then I could simply wash my own plate.

I started at the sound of Auntie Beatrice's voice.

'If people want to eat at any hour they please they can always go to a restaurant.' I apologized meekly, saying that I hadn't known we were eating earlier. Auntie Beatrice continued as if I had never spoken.

'Nobody can say I haven't tried, God is my witness I have tried. But what can you do, what? Who can undo the work of the Devil? And what have I got for my trouble, what? If it wasn't my own flesh and blood so help me Almighty I would give up. Huh! My own flesh and blood! Who would think so? Anybody who didn't know would say it was some family with no kind of background, nobody would believe there was good blood. But give the sons of kings to pigs and they will turn into pigs. Ah, yes!' Auntie Beatrice sighed dramatically. I was feeding myself mechanically, tasting nothing. With one prong of my fork I was spearing up single grains of rice. 'God rest her soul and give her peace they might just as well have put them in the Orphanage, it would have been no greater shame. What could they turn into but little ragamuffins with no manners and no gratitude. What a mercy she took the last with her, what a mercy Mary Mother of God, not another infant delivered into the hands of a fallen woman. And may God forgive her for the two she brought into the world.'

23

One day when I came home from school there lay on the dining-table an envelope covered with the tendril growth that was Tantie's hand, addressed to me. At the sight of it a freezing dismay swarmed into my insides. The letter ran:

Dear Cyntie,
    Not a word you write to your Tan-Tan since April why is that. Toddan is fine he is in Secon Standard now you know. Dularie is also fine she said Tantie I keeping you company till Cyn-Cyn come back. Well now why I am writing this letter is. I am sure you will be glad to hear of it we are coming to see you Friday evening so tell that bitch so she could please herself. We are getting a drop in Uncle Sylvester's car you remember Uncle Sylvester.
                                        Yours truly,
                                        Tantie.

With horror I realized that it was Friday. There was no chance of warding them off and who were 'them' I suddenly thought, my heart making one more plunge towards my stomach, who was Tantie bringing here to Auntie Beatrice's house?

Coweringly I broke the news to Auntie Beatrice.

'Oh my good Heavens, and Father is coming today!' she made for the telephone. One of Auntie Beatrice's social triumphs was that Father Sheridan came at least once a fortnight and lounged in our drawingroom, letting himself be pampered and fussed about with tea and cake and more than a drop of whisky or brandy. Auntie Beatrice was saying on the phone that something *rorther* unexpected had turned up and couldn't Forther please come another day.

◆

I waited in pain for the sound of a car drawing up at our gate. Carol and Jessica were agog with wicked expectation; Auntie Beatrice moved about the house with her worst dragon-face on. Several times I nearly fainted at the sound of a car braking. But when they came they stood darkening the front door before I was aware of anything.

Auntie Beatrice withdrew pointedly inside with a 'Hm!' Carol and Jessica I knew were stationing themselves behind doors and curtains as they did when Roger Hernandez was in the drawing-room with Bernadette.

'Tee! Dou-dou!' Tantie swept into the drawingroom with the whole band in tow. Horrors, they had brought Doolarie, what would Auntie Beatrice say to that afterwards? And Uncle Sylvester coarse and repulsive, his over-fed stomach tipping out over the top of his pants. They sat themselves down as though they had every right to make themselves comfortable in these surroundings. In fact the tone of Auntie Beatrice's drawingroom did not seem to make the slightest impression on them.

Toddan had lost some of his roundness, he was a boy. Doolarie was in her yellow dress, and the white shoes, and the fronts had already been cut away to give her toes room. She

117

stood leaning against Tantie's knees with her silent, large-eyed gaze fixed upon me. Once Tantie held her and coaxed: 'Well look Cyn-Cyn, talk to her, nuh, dou-dou! All the things yu had to tell her!' and Doolarie, overcome with shyness, buried her head in Tantie's lap.

I realized afterwards that I had sat on the edge of my chair for the whole time, with my head hung. The worst moment of all was when they drew forth a series of greasy paper bags, announcing that they contained polorie, anchar, roti from Neighb' Ramlaal-Wife, and accra and fry-bake and zaboca from Tantie, with a few other things I had almost forgotten existed, in short, all manner of ordinary nastiness. I could picture the other two giggling helplessly in their hiding-places.

As I sat with the bags poised gingerly on my knee Tantie suggested: 'Well yu don' want to eat a polorie or something? What yu waitin for?' I declined in alarm: the very thought of sitting in Auntie Beatrice's drawingroom eating coolie-food! And *accra*! *Saltfish*! Fancy even bringing saltfish into Auntie Beatrice's house! When I refused Uncle Sylvester, to my disgust, leaned over and said familiarly: 'Awright, dou-dou, lemme help yu out them,' and reaching into a greasy bag drew out a thick spotted roti; he settled back with sounds of satisfaction and opening his jaws wide enough to accommodate Government House (this was a dictum of Auntie Beatrice's in the context of table-manners) proceeded to champ away. A strong smell of curry assailed the drawingroom. That was another thing I would pay for afterwards, I thought miserably. And I hoped Auntie Beatrice wasn't looking on too, with Uncle Sylvester sitting on the sofa eating roti and curry with as much reverence as if he were sitting on a tapia-floor.

Toddan talked steadily, and it was when he had delivered all the news and dried up that it must have dawned on Tantie that I hadn't really had very much to say for myself. But perhaps I under-rated Tantie; she didn't take her eyes off me the whole time, and the few times that I dared look her way I was unable to read her expression.

Then suddenly she sprang to her feet, gathered Doolarie and Toddan while Uncle Sylvester eased his mass up slowly, sighing disgustingly (just like a niggerman, I thought), and announced abruptly: 'We goin now, Cyntie, tell yu Auntie Beatrice we gone.'

And she kissed me on my forehead, turned and hustled the children out.

As they disappeared through the door I had one fleeting urge to call them back.

24

Several times in the next few weeks I contemplated running away and going back to Tantie. I worked it out in great detail – the bus to the railway station, the train to Coriaca and then the bus that would put me down at Ramsaran's corner. I had money. I would just have to leave the house normally one morning and instead of going to school go to the bus-depot and ask which bus went to the station. People on the train might find it strange that a girl in St Ann's uniform was heading out of town at that hour of the day. They might think I was breaking biche. But I could look sick so that they would think I'd taken ill and had to go home again. I didn't need any baggage because I had clothes up there. And Tantie would soon make me some more.

Then I would be getting off the bus at Ramsaran's corner and I would meet all kinds of people on Tucunu Road. Maybe I would meet some of my classmates from EC School, the ones who had not got to secondary school and who regarded me as a kind of heroine for having gotten into St Ann's.

I would cross the bridge and the boys might be sitting there, and they would say in surprise 'A-a! Cyntie? Wha'yu doin here, girl?' Further up the road Ma-Philippa's disagreeable dog, if it wasn't dead yet, would start its frantic barking as I approached the chennette tree and keep it up until I had passed the hedge.

Sooner or later I would be at the front gate. And it was always here that my plan broke down. For here I stood and looked up the path and saw Tantie standing in the gallery with her arms folded.

Then, crazily, I thought of making my way up to Pointe d'Espoir instead. Ma would surely welcome me with bursting joy. She would make me sit down and stuff myself, while Junie and Yvie and all the others stood around and eyed me with respect, if Ma allowed them in at all. Then we would go for a walk and she would hail all the people out of their houses to see her 'Tee and what a big girl she had grown into. Then we would come home again, up the track, up the wooden steps into the house with the cane-bottomed chairs and the dark cabinet with curly legs. And then we would sit down facing each other; and the picture stubbornly snuffed itself out.

Pointe d'Espoir might have been on the other side of the earth, and I awoke again even more brutally into Auntie Beatrice's house, with the smell of floor-polish in the drawingroom and the smell of shampoo in the bathroom somehow mixed up with Bernadette's voice floating down the front path: 'Oh that's some lil relative Mommer found up in the country.'

◆

Then one day when I came home from school Auntie Beatrice almost ran down the front path to greet me. She was beaming and beside herself, and she could hardly contain the news; she had got a letter from Tantie saying that my father was sending two plane tickets for Toddan and me and we were to leave at the end of the term.

The last time my father had suggested we join him Tantie had been on the rampage for a week of evenings.

◆

In the remaining time my standing was like that of a pariah who has suddenly inherited a title. Carol and Jessica regarded me with mute awe. Auntie Beatrice threw a party for me and invited all the nice people's children she could think of, so that the news got safely around to all the nice people. She took me shopping for clothes and managed to communicate to every shop-clerk that this was her little niece who was going up to England so we were just getting a few things together, you know. And to my astonishment I one day overheard Bernadette in the gallery relating to her friends: 'She is our first cousin. Her mother died so she's been living with us – and she is so bright at school! She goes to St Ann's with Carol, you know, and she came *first* in the last test. . . .'

Mrs Wattman detained me after class and interrogated me with the same besotted expression she had on her face when she probed some of the girls in the class with questions about their mummies and daddies.

'What a lucky girl you are!' she cooed, 'but tell me, how long has your daddy been up there?'

'About seven years.'

'Seven years! But you never told us, you naughty girl, you never told us your daddy was abroad!'

◆

121

I went up to Santa Clara almost at the last minute. With all the springy air I was treading there were thoughts that maliciously kept returning to trip me up and dash me face downwards to the hard earth. I did not relish facing Tantie again. It was strange that she had written to Auntie Beatrice and not to me, and why were we going up to my father anyway, was Tantie giving us over without a fight? And was it pure coincidence that my father should ask for us now, when the last time had been almost two years ago? Again and again I dismissed the conclusion that this time it was not my father who had asked Tantie to send us up to him.

Everyone piled into the car to take me home, even Bernadette. The bakery, the bridge, the immortelle tree all these landmarks that had filled me with elation the last time I had come home from Auntie Beatrice were now about as exciting to me as benches in a waitingroom.

I need not have worried about Tantie's reception. Tantie's head was tied and for the moment there was no sting in her. For Ma had died the week before. She informed me, and every word was a ton of bricks on my head, that Ma had been asking for Tee, Tee, but that she had told her that Tee had no time to come all the way up to Pointe d'Espoir to see her; in the last days Ma had suddenly remembered her grandmother's name and wanted it to be added to my names. Tantie hadn't even bothered to remember it.

Everything was changing, unrecognizable, pushing me out. This was as it should be, since I had moved up and no longer had any place here. But it was painful, and I longed all the more to be on my way. Ma gone; the shaddock tree dried up as if with Mikey gone it no longer had any function; Tantie had taken one of Mikey's little sisters who was wearing my clothes, two of Ma's children and to all intents and purposes Doolarie for Ramlaal had been involved in a serious accident with the truck and was going to be in hospital for a long time.

122

The night before we left the macommès and compès filled the house, come to drink a little one on us. But macommès and compès are never known to stop at a little one, and the usual gaiety ensued, in which we the pretext were quite forgotten. Which was just as well, for I sat in a corner shrinking from the ordinaryness of it all, until Mr Joseph pounced on me.

'A-a Cyntie girl, come and dance for the last – they don' do much o' that whe' allyu goin, yu know, come dance, man!'

Tantie was mirthlessly drunk. And then suddenly she tottered to the middle of the room, clapping her hands.

'Hush everybody hush! Speech-time, speech-time! Hush allyu tail lemme make the goin'-away speech. Brethren we are gathered here . . . but what the arse I talkie? Gimmie some rum allyu, I ain' talkin so good. . . . Well now the speech we have to make is, to wish God-bless to my chirren – ' Tantie stopped and her face grew thoughtful. 'But why they must take mih chirren, what it is I do them at-all?' Then she giggled briefly as she tottered back to her seat: 'Hee. Drink an' spread joy allyu, for my chirren is goin unto the Golden Gates.' Her face seemed to slump: 'Drink one on Rosa, she takin she own chirren an sendin them up in the cold, for what to do?'

I desired with all my heart that it were next morning and a plane were lifting me off the ground.

Study Questions

1. Express in your own words the central theme of *Crick Crack, Monkey*?

2. Illustrate in detail the contrast Merle Hodge presents through the characters of Aunt Beatrice and Tantie.

3. Outline the development of Tee/Cynthia from the period of her early upbringing with Tantie to the time when she becomes assimilated into the world of Aunt Beatrice.

4. Identify those characteristics of childhood and schooling that are presented in the novel. Refer to specific incidents and situations to support your answer.

5. Discuss the nature of the relationship between:
   (a) Tee and Aunt Beatrice
   (b) Tee and Tantie.

6. Imagine you are the author of *Crick Crack, Monkey*. Prepare a statement of your purpose/intention in writing this novel.

7. Select two or three scenes from the novel for dramatic presentation. Make sure to select those scenes which reveal situations of either conflict or humour.

8. 'The novel in its general impact is both disturbing and delightful.' Discuss this statement by detailing your general response to certain parts of the novel.